# Laugh More

STORIES FROM
AN UNEXPECTED LIFE

# DEBBIE TRAVIS

ILLUSTRATIONS
BY LISA BRANCATISANO

RANDOM HOUSE CANADA

PUBLISHED BY RANDOM HOUSE CANADA

www.penguinrandomhouse.ca

Random House Canada and colophon are registered trademarks.

Library and Archives Canada Cataloguing in Publication

Title: Laugh more : stories from an unexpected life / Debbie Travis.
Names: Travis, Debbie, author.
Description: Includes index.
Identifiers: Canadiana (print) 20240350677 | Canadiana (ebook) 20240350758 | ISBN 9781039009332 (hardcover) | ISBN 9781039009349 (EPUB)
Subjects: LCSH: Travis, Debbie—Anecdotes. | LCSH: Travis, Debbie—Family—Anecdotes. | LCSH: Interior decorators—Canada—Anecdotes. | LCSH: Television personalities—Canada—Anecdotes. | LCGFT: Anecdotes.
Classification: LCC NK2013.Z9 T73 2024 | DDC 747.092—dc23

Jacket and interior design: Lisa Jager
Typesetting: Daniella Zanchetta
Illustrations: Lisa Brancatisano

Printed in the United States of America

10 9 8 7 6 5 4 3 2 1

Penguin
Random House
RANDOM HOUSE CANADA

This book is dedicated to everyone who is in desperate need of a good laugh. And, always, to Hans, my best friend, therapist, agent, list follower, daily-drama fixer, washer-upper, bedmaker and the person who always makes *me* laugh. And to my loves, Josh, Max, Fiona, Andy and Billie the border collie.

# CONTENTS

"There is something about laughter that
can take away all the darkness."
—CHRISTINA APPLEGATE

# Introduction

It is hard to nail down exactly when I told my first story, but I do remember the first time I captured an audience. I think I was about eight the day I arrived home from school in my usually dishevelled fluster and barged into the living room, where my mother was entertaining her girlfriends over afternoon tea. Breathless, I told the women how George, the naughtiest boy in the class, had climbed onto the top shelf in the library while our teacher, round Mrs. Ramsbottom, who looked like a bee in her yellow trousers and black blouse, was reading to us. The teacher tried her best to ignore George, but then he slipped and landed on top of Helen the hamster's cage. Both he and Helen escaped injury, but the cage was damaged and the hamster ran off! I paused there and took in the room, making sure I had their full attention.

And then the finale: hysteria reigned in the classroom. Chairs fell over as all the girls climbed up on their desks, skirts tucked into their knickers. The boys, including George, were down on their hands and knees, searching for Helen the hamster. Suddenly, a tremendous roar boomed from the doorway, causing us all to jump. The headmaster, Mr. Turnbull, whom even the teachers were terrified of, stood there red-faced while Mrs. Ramsbottom, sobbing into her handkerchief, explained the situation to him.

"Nobody move," he bellowed, "except for you, Debbie. Go and fetch the janitor."

I don't remember if Helen was caught, but I do remember tingling with pleasure as my mother's friends shrieked and gasped. My mother laughed too. I loved to make her laugh.

Since then, I have thrived on being a storyteller, a minstrel entertaining a crowd. What's not to love about telling a delightful tale? For me, sharing spicy snippets the morning after a party is as delicious as diving into last night's leftovers.

It doesn't matter whether I'm speaking to an audience of one or a conference of a thousand women, I always feel the itch to share a funny experience. Before a day's filming on my own series or as a guest on other people's shows, I'm filled with anxiety and self-doubt. But once I am in the moment, the tales tumble forth. In life, my favourite thing may just be making others laugh, and I find it comes in handy too. Through five television shows and eleven books, I taught the art and craft of design, and later lifestyle and wellness. To my mind, there is nothing more boring than advice or instruction delivered straight. But if you build a story as you go—around the nervous family whose home you are smashing apart, the nosy neighbour who keeps popping in to give advice, the neurotic relatives worried that they are being one-upped—the viewer will be not only entertained but engaged, taking in everything you hoped to show them. But it won't work unless it's a *good* story, and it'll work even better if it's funny!

I learned the art of embellishing a yarn with humour while sprawled at my mother's feet.

My mum was young, beautiful and exhausted, but she came alive when she told an entertaining tale. Her eyes shone with mischief and the stern lines of the mouth that kept us kids in line would soften as she spoke, her storytelling an escape from the mundane chores of family life and the hand that dealt her widowhood in her mid-thirties. It wasn't hard to notice that she usually slanted her tales away from the truth, for the sole purpose of making us laugh. Our joy was her prescription to carry on.

As a storyteller, she was good, but she had nothing on her mother, my granny. Lose the image of a blue-rinsed old lady, her knitting on her lap, sipping a lovely cuppa. Oh no, my granny, who was not old—at most in her early fifties when I was a teenager; she'd given birth to my mum at fifteen—oozed glamour and naughtiness. Joyce, which is what we kids called her, was a Northerner just like us, but she lived half the year on the French Riviera, claiming she needed the warm, dry climate for medicinal reasons. We never quite knew what these were. But the medicine must have worked, because she died a week shy of her ninetieth birthday. And she might have carried on to a hundred, maybe accumulating another of her many husbands, if she'd still been living in France rather than on the seafront in Morecambe, Lancashire, which is notorious for its blustery winds. Nipping to the shops one morning, she was whisked off her feet by a wild gust that deposited her on the hood of a police car. She died a few days later.

For twenty years or more, Joyce had fled south to the Côte d'Azur, waving goodbye to the cold English drizzle. She never flew, not because she was afraid of crashing but because she'd heard that airplane food was dreadful. Instead, she drove. Behind the wheel of her beat-up Volkswagen Beetle, she perched her tiny frame on a pile of cushions so she could see through the windscreen. She was an atrocious driver who should have been banned from the roads. Keeping one arm free to gesture rudely to any motorist unlucky enough to be in her vicinity, and clutching the steering wheel with the other, our own Cruella de Vil somehow survived the two-thousand-kilometre drive from Morecambe to Monte Carlo, an inhabitant of two worlds that could not have been more different.

Joyce was not the only expat lapping up life on the fashionable beaches and in the elegant towns perched along the French Riviera. Nice, Monte Carlo, Cannes and Saint Tropez, all playgrounds of the rich and the glamorous, were in their heyday in the 1960s and '70s. The Brits fortunate enough to be able to indulge in a trip abroad fled their homeland's nastier seasons, desperate to soak up the Mediterranean sun, sea and endless cocktail parties, following in the footsteps of the aristocrats of earlier centuries, who had been the first to seek a gentler climate for their health; the seven-kilometre, palm-lined Promenade des Anglais in Nice is named after them. While my grandmother may have insisted that she went south for her health, she actually went for the parties, especially long afternoons sipping gin and tonic on terraces surrounded by lush vegetation, and the gossip, which was her forte.

Joyce loved to emboss slices of other people's lives with a mix of both sympathy and glittering wit. No matter how many times she told the same story, which was countless, she always added a new twist. Though she was not a drinker, in the social whirl of the Côte d'Azur, not to partake was frowned upon, so she faked it. She could nurse a solitary gin for hours, giving the impression she was as tipsy as the rest of the party, a ruse that enabled her to witness and remember the absurdities of the flamboyant, the fascinating and the dreadful bores. Then she would bring her scandalous tales home to our comfy English living room and shock the knickers off us (though she did try to keep her accounts of the more colourful incidents relatively clean in front of us kids).

A Joyce classic was the one about the old movie star who'd cornered her at a wealthy sheikh's soiree in Cap Ferrat. Perched at the bar, she'd listened as he tediously rattled on about his performance in a particular Hollywood movie that later garnered him a global award. We didn't care about that—it was what he was doing while he mused to Joyce that had us in stitches every time. As the old egomaniac droned on and on about his achievements, he guzzled his way through a couple of oversized glasses of cognac, all the while munching from a large dish of what must have looked to him like dried seeds and nuts. Finally, he'd used a sausage-like finger to wipe the bowl clean of any last bits. After unleashing a loud and perfumed belch, he declared to my grandmother that the snack was tasteless and dreadfully dry. Joyce smiled sweetly. She'd watched him polish off an entire bowl of potpourri.

Even now that story makes me both howl with laughter and miss her dreadfully.

Every storyteller needs a good foundation for her tales. For the last ten years, mine has been the upheaval that led to me changing everything I'd been doing with my life and fulfilling my dream of moving to Italy. Mind you, when I first saw the crumbling ruin of the Tuscan farmhouse that has become our home, I told my hubby, Hans, "I am *not* living here." How wrong I was.

The journey to our new life began with a policeman sitting on my knee during my surprise fiftieth birthday party in Montreal. I'd imagined a simple affair to mark this milestone, maybe a dinner out with a few buddies. Definitely not a surprise party. Then a truck laden with scaffolding backed down the driveway, beeping loudly. Hans had booked caterers and a fully stocked bar, arranged for flowers and music and managed to cram a shiny white stage into our small city garden. He'd smuggled family members in from England and put them up in a nearby hotel, and also recruited friends and colleagues in his attempt to surprise me. Flabbergasted and absolutely thrilled that he had gone to all this trouble, I made sure to feign shock when the partygoers arrived that evening. The party was epic, raucous and wonderful. So raucous and wonderful, in fact, that as we danced towards midnight, a neighbour called the police. But instead of shutting us down, the officers joined in—it may have helped that I'd decorated the local police station's kitchen for one of my television shows.

Then an inebriated someone suggested that I have my birthday portrait taken with a young and rather handsome copper sitting on my knee. Hmmm. Laughing, he perched precariously, trying not to squash me. I looked out on a hundred people in full-on party mode, and my world smiled back at me. Amongst the crowd were my sons, back from university, my husband, my siblings, friends from school, friends from London and members of the television tribe I'd worked alongside for years. I felt immensely grateful and loved in that moment, but I also felt a shift—a premonition of the future—and a wave of excitement came over me (not caused by the young policeman, who had hopped off my knee and was back on the dance floor). It was as if I could see the whole blueprint of my life as it was that day—each room in the floor plan representing a piece of my past and present. There was the kitchen, standing for all the years I spent mothering my lads, both of whom were rarely home now since the elder was at university in England, the younger at school in France. The bedroom, well, that would be Hans and me. There were other rooms for work (too many of those) and a room for play. And in that moment, I thought: What if I crumpled up the old floor plan and started from scratch—tossed aside all that was familiar and comfortable and followed the dream Hans and I had been hanging on to for a while? A home in Italy.

It had been only a dream for two good reasons: not enough money and a reluctance to uproot our children. What made this moment different? Age, possibly. To me, at the time, fifty seemed ancient. (Ha!) I was at the top of my game in the lifestyle genre I'd helped to pioneer, but I also felt I had done everything and more: television shows, books, a home products collection and a syndicated column that appeared in nearly a hundred different newspapers all across North America. My chosen home had been good to me, but was there more of the world to explore? As the clock edged past midnight, I knew I was ready to begin the search for whatever was beckoning us in Italy.

The next day, as the wreckage and remnants of my birthday party were being hauled away, I told Hans about my vision of crumpling up our old floor plan. This is one of the many reasons my marriage to Hans has been so long-lasting: when I said it was time to launch into something new, he not only agreed but said he'd been ready for a while. He was just waiting for me.

—

Why was Italy our dream when we had no connection of any sort to the country? Like so many who visit, we'd fallen in love.

I'd taken the occasional trip to Italy with my grandmother, who spent her winters on the Menton side of the French/Italian border, but Hans and I began to explore the country together while we were filming my first television series, *The Painted House*. The show had been an overnight success in Canada and the United States, and quickly sold to over eighty countries. As a result, the production budget grew, enabling us to film abroad, where I would be inspired by a variety of decorating styles in each place we travelled. I would then recreate that look in someone's home. There were Caribbean, Adirondack and American Shaker styles, English Gothic and the wonders of Renaissance Italy. But it was the travels in Italy that became life-changing for Hans and me. We were enamoured with the land, the people, the food and of course the wine. Vision boards went up in my basement as I tried out the "law of attraction." If I pinned up a magazine page with a picture of a Florentine villa, would it become mine?

Jumping forward, we are now living that dream. There were countless hilarious moments while we searched for the perfect place and settled into this foreign life, but it has turned out that everyday life here on a hillside in Tuscany is always a roller-coaster ride. One I'm really looking forward to taking you on.

As the stories and the Tuscan seasons unfolded through a year in my life, they also sparked a whole load of memories that catapulted me back to my childhood in the north of England, my debauched London life as a model, my TV career and raising our sons. The stories are literally all over the map! Most of all, I hope they make you laugh.

# Winter

> "Wisdom comes with winters."
>
> —OSCAR WILDE

# A New Year in Tuscany

Winter arrives slowly this year, as if it wants to apologize for the increasing nip in the air. Though the early mornings are crisp, the heavy jackets still loiter in the closet.

People tend to assume that when January comes—the retreats over, guests gone—Hans and I cuddle up for the season, taking time for ourselves. Oh, how I wish. Once the holiday festivities are finished, the hangovers departed, the decorations packed away until next year and the diets and best intentions showing their unwanted faces, we take on the interminable repairs that keep Villa Reniella beautiful—painting and plastering where suitcases have bashed the walls and mending any broken furniture or fittings. Now is also the time of year when I have the time to think up larger projects. As each winter settles in, I dive into what I want to add to our paradise next—a cutting garden here, a meditation platform there. Hans does his best to close his ears to my persistent chirping along the lines of "I may grow potatoes this year, or what if we add another eating area, or what about extending the patio?" But I always wear him down.

This year, our big project is going to be a vast extension to the main terrace.

For centuries before we got here, Villa Reniella was a working farm. After five years of intense renovation, we managed to morph it from a home for pigs and chickens into a villa. Umberto, the lanky, blue-blooded Italian architect who was glued to my hip throughout the renovation and rebuilding, looked down his aristocratic nose when I added the prefix *Villa* to the farm's name, which was Reniella.

"It is not a villa," he scoffed. "It is a *podere*." To him, once a farm, always a farm, no matter how we dressed it up. Villas are signs of prestige and wealth, and, Umberto insisted, I had neither.

"I really don't care," I said. "I have spent my life savings on this pile of stone, and I will call it a *castello* if I so desire!"

That was pushing it, given that our home does not resemble a castle by any means. So villa it was.

A little note: Italian villas—country estates, often with numerous outbuildings—date back to the Roman Empire. A villa is truly what I intended this dilapidated farm to become. Still, Umberto had a point: it was a long road from *podere* to here. He is a superb architect with an impeccable fashion sense that was irrelevant and annoying on a building site, but invaluable when it came to the essential task of charming the ladies in the permit office. We'd chosen him after we visited a real castle that he'd tastefully restored to its eleventh-century glory—his work seduced us. Then he and I proceeded to argue over every single decision for the next five years.

When we bought the place, there was a main farmhouse with stables on the ground floor. The workers and their families had lived upstairs, and the animals down below. Then there was the barn, a brutally ugly structure that we converted so that it resembles a fancy stable on the outside but inside houses designer suites and a communal lounge and kitchen. The third and last building was a sprawling series of cement pigsties—or, in Italian, the *porcellia*. (Guests look downtrodden when I announce they'll be sleeping in a pigsty. *Porcellia* sounds so much more romantic.)

Large chunks of Tuscany are protected from development. In areas of great beauty, such as the Val d'Orcia, which is the valley we overlook, it is painfully difficult—well, actually, impossible—to add new buildings to your property, or even to change the roof lines and the size of the original windows on the existing ones. The contortions you have to undergo to make even the slightest change to a historic building are about as painful as grabbing a scalpel and operating on yourself. The local bureaucrat we had to deal with believed her job was to turn down every request from a baffled foreigner who had the audacity to think she could restore a property in Tuscany. She loathed me. I am convinced she watched out the window as I parked my car, her rubber stamp already quivering above the permit forms. On a weekly basis I would walk through her office door and the NO stamp would immediately thump down on my application. NO, thump, to the request of changing the size of an existing window. NO, thump, to the absurd idea of shrinking the overly wide entrance built for cattle to the size of a practical doorway. NO. NO. NO.

When I applied to add a wrought-iron Juliet balcony, with visions of cascading geraniums, she turned scarlet, as if I had asked permission to marry her dog, and pointed at the door. A neighbour had painted the outside plasterwork of his converted barn a deep blood red. I applied to do the same—NO. When I begged Umberto to reason with her, she screamed at him too.

Apparently, the neighbour's house was on the other side of the road, which meant it was in a different *comune*. Certain *ufficio permessi* around here would not even allow a swimming pool. Luckily, we received a *Sì* stamp to this courageous request, as long as it was not blue or used for swimming!

But there is rhyme and reason to this madness: it's why much of the Tuscan landscape still resembles a Renaissance painting. Which is one of the reasons our paying guests love to come here so much.

Paying guests? Wait! What happened to finding a home somewhere in Italy, one that we could retreat to on holidays or just when we needed a rest? Well, we did spend several years searching for exactly that (more about this later). But somewhere along the way, I became intrigued by the beneficial ways in which time spent in Italy affected my health and happiness, and I decided to share my Italian home with others by turning our villa into a retreat and oasis.

So, instead of a place all to ourselves, we live in the main villa, in a home that is also a small hotel, with fourteen guest suites, massage huts, a kitchen garden, a swimming pool, a pond and a yoga platform. After we demolished the barn and pigsties, we rebuilt them on the same footprint, turning them into the suites, and then we reinvented the farmhouse, including adding a kitchen with an enormous centre island around which a crowd of women can gather over glasses of Prosecco to learn the art of pasta-making. On top of all that, we terraced the surrounding hilly land into gardens. Our hundred acres includes several olive orchards, a chestnut and oak forest, and a stream—and it also came with a pensioner who, for forty years, had farmed a small *campo*, or lot, on our land, where he raised rabbits, chickens, fruit and vegetables for his family. What were we to do with *him*?

We asked around and found that inheriting a person is a common predicament when buying property in Italy. Swiss friends told us that when they purchased a house on a tired old farm and were spending their first night there, camped out on the ground floor, they heard movement upstairs. They investigated and discovered an eighty-year-old man. The next day they called the previous owner, who told them, "Oh, that's Granddad! We forgot to mention that he comes with the place." The young Swiss couple had no choice but to embrace this old man, which turned out to be a good thing. In return, he taught them everything he knew about sustainable farming, and he ended up staying on with them until he died.

Another friend put it wisely: "Do you need that patch of land? If not, carry on the way it has always been, and let change come when it is ready."

Not only did Simone and his wife continue to work their *campo*, but they delivered regular gifts of fresh eggs and plastic bags filled with blooded rabbit limbs (horrifying to look at, but they do make for a good stock!). Finally, the day came when he told us he was moving away to live with his children in the warmer south. Now that he was too frail to work the land, he was handing it back to us. The rhythm of life! It often works out in the end.

We kick off January, as planned, with the building of the new terrace, a humongous job. If we'd widened the terrace that runs along the south-facing side of the villa when the initial renovation was taking place—as I'd wanted to do—it would have been a straightforward affair. But Umberto had insisted the authorities would allow it to be only so wide, and I peevishly succumbed.

Since then, I have learned to be more Italian and ignore the rules. The trouble is that, with the entire property finished, there is no way for large equipment to access the area where the extended terrace will be built.

When the contractor and the stonemasons arrive, they engage in a long and animated discussion over numerous espressos and walnut cake. This is the Tuscan way. Arms get flung in the air, gestures indicate that someone is crazy (that would be me), and then magic happens—they find a solution and the work begins.

In this case, they first need to pour concrete footings and a foundation on which to build a three-metre-high retaining wall. And it can't be just any old wall. Due to the mind-numbing rules and regulations of renovating a property in a protected area, the wall must resemble the ancient stone structures of a bygone era.

Claudio and Luca, our stonemasons, are brothers who resemble characters in a children's book: Luca, skinny and sullen; Claudio, round and jolly. They have built every exterior wall at Villa Reniella. Walls that terrace the land, walls that hold up the buildings, walls that required restoring, and outbuilding walls that needed to be rebuilt from scratch to look as if they had been here for centuries.

We're ready for them. Ramps have been built and a small crane has hoisted the heavier equipment into place. But before any work begins—before trucks of butter-coloured stones are unloaded and before the cement mixer, which has been dragged through my lavender beds, is booted into life—the inevitable conversation takes place. Luca asks, "Where do we set up for lunch?" As he and his brother discuss the dilemma, I see them staring at the massage hut. I crumble with despair. With no guests around, I've been intending to repurpose it as a writing hut, where I would be far enough away from Hans's constant questions about what's for lunch and whether we are out of loo roll that I'd be able to concentrate. I planned to replace the massage table with a desk and chair. The shelf that usually displays body oils would be for my research and drafts.

No such luck. Soon the brothers have hauled in a set of rickety chairs, a microwave oven, a kettle, and a tablecloth to throw over the massage table—all the makings of a clubhouse typical of a builders' site anywhere. (The tablecloth, probably, being exclusive to Italy.)

As with all my plans for life in Italy, I have had to make a major U-turn before I even got started. You'll now find me tucked away and writing in a broom cupboard in the villa, rather than "a hut with a view."

"People don't notice whether it's winter
or summer when they're happy."
—ANTON CHEKHOV

# An Unexpected Blizzard

The blossoming of the almond trees in late January always takes me unawares. Every year I say to myself, *Surely it's too early and too cold,* but there they are again, lightly blushed buds appearing amongst the leafless branches. Soon they will open into white blossoms with a magenta centre, releasing a scent that is sweet and sensual.

The buds put a much-needed spring in my step. On top of the work in and around the villa, we are preparing the farmland and gardens for all the guests who will stay with us from spring until the olive and grape harvests in late fall.

The olive trees have been so rigorously pruned they resemble boys with brutally short haircuts on their first day of school. With last season's grape harvest happily fermenting away in large vats, on the way to becoming another batch of our lethal wine, we've cut the vines back to stubby stems. And we still have to deal with the badly behaved member of the family: the pond I had dug against all advice. Once again it needs to be drained because of the evil smell oozing from the green slime that is slowly creeping across the surface, promising the dreaded lurgies to anyone who may fancy a dip.

If you'd told me or Hans we'd be farmers in our autumnal years, we would have shrieked with horrified disbelief. Not us—we're sophisticated television people, city folk!

Mind you, as a teenager I seemed doomed to be a farmer's wife. Though I now hold this way of life in high esteem, I certainly didn't when I was a gangly sixteen-year-old in what turned out to be the last months of my formal education. My final school report stated: "Travis has little aptitude for further studies (or sitting still). She'd be better off finding factory work or farming. She does have a keen eye for the arts." Since my mother saw a career in the arts as futureless and hadn't ever pictured me in university—in those days relatively few students in my area in the north of England pursued higher education—she gladly accepted my decision to leave home. One less mouth to feed. I always knew there was something bigger and better than the village where I was brought up, and I had an escape plan—the number 44 bus to Manchester, followed by the train to London. When the day came, my mother handed me the bus and train fare and a cheese sandwich to hold me for the eight-hour trip, then gave me a quick hug and told me to behave. That was it. A field day for social workers today, but those were very different times.

At least the weather is cooperating for all the outside work. As global temperatures rise, Italy is having drier springs and longer, sizzling summers. Even in the heart of winter, if it's warm enough, we often dine alfresco. But that is not always the case. During the retreats here, I get a kick out of sharing pictures of our mammoth renovation. Like a comedian, I can forecast where the laughs and the astonished gasps will come as each image pops up on the screen, telling the tale of the construction from collapsed farm to fancy villa. The pictures that receive the biggest gasps of disbelief are those of me and the workers knee-deep in snow.

Inevitably, someone cries out, "You have snow here?"

"Occasionally," I tell them.

True, snow is rare in the Val d'Orcia, but just after we made the decision to buy Reniella, we were hit with a catastrophic blizzard that nearly had us ripping up our brand-new deed of sale and moving to a tropical island.

Our final real estate adventure got off to a rocky start. As I've said, my first glimpse of the rundown working farm that became our villa and retreat was not inspiring: mud-sloshed yards in which pigs and chickens wandered, ugly outbuildings, ramshackle pigsties and a couple of oak trees growing up and through the roof of the farmhouse. This was the place Hans had insisted I had to fly to Italy to see in the middle of a ruthless shooting schedule?

"You must be kidding—it's a ruin," I ranted. "I am *not* living here."

Instead of arguing the case, Hans calmly said, "Be quiet and look at that view."

I did as I was told, and realized once again that my sweet, kind husband knows me well. I turned and stared out at a scene unchanged for centuries, one understandably loved by artists, poets and filmmakers. Reniella is perched on a slope, like Humpty Dumpty on his wall. The land tumbles away to a forest and stream, then lifts up again into the quintessential hills of Tuscany, carpeted with vineyards and olive groves and fields of wheat. Cypress trees, tall, slim and elegant, fringe each horizon. Across the valley is the Renaissance hilltop town of Montepulciano, clearly visible from where I stood. Later, I learned the town was originally an Etruscan settlement whose people lived in caves and worshipped pagan gods. Garrisons of Romans eventually marched in and wiped them out, and as a result it's a civilization we know little about. Around here, though, you can easily see traces of the Romans. An original Roman road runs through the village of Montefollonico, at the top of our hill, an historic artefact that the locals helped excavate with their biggest kitchen spoons. I have been staring at this view for years now, and feel I am always learning something new.

But back then, I sighed deeply and put my arm around Hans. He was right.

The potential of the property was screaming from its ravaged rooftops. My every nerve ending tingled with anticipation. This was our future.

It was mid-December when the moment finally came to shake hands on the deal. Reniella was ours, but we would need to return in the new year to complete the rest of the interminable paperwork. The old owners waved us off, smirking as they tried to hide their elation at finally unloading the ancestral home on us gullible

foreigners, happy about their upcoming move to a new apartment with all the mod cons and a roof that didn't have trees growing through it!

We, too, were grinning—at last we were homeowners in Tuscany. We whizzed down country roads, winding our way through the iconic landscape, our destination the airport in Florence, where we'd catch a flight to London for Christmas with our family. The sky was vivid blue, the winter sun shimmering over gently sloping hills of olive orchards. Pastures of clover, alongside fields of turned soil, were a beautiful patchwork of purple and nutty brown.

We were both thinking that life could not be better, until a stooped old geezer at the side of the road frantically waved his stick at us.

"Strange," Hans muttered, and on we roared.

Seconds later, another local signalled us to slow down, and then another. Was there an accident ahead or something?

Suddenly, day turned to night. Billowing snow clouds blanketed the sun, and before we could scream "What! It snows in Tuscany?!" snowflakes the size of tennis balls were angrily slapping the windscreen. I clutched the dashboard as Hans, no longer smiling, manoeuvred the dinky rental car on the now slippery road, a vein on his forehead standing out and his jaw set in concentration. The cypress trees loomed over us, ghostly figures in the gloom. Soon the vineyards and everything else around us were covered in white icing, eerie and silent. Visibility was diddly-squat. The only thing to be grateful for was that, when the storm hit, we were only a kilometre from the highway. Carefully crawling along, we finally made it to the gas station at our exit.

"Once we are on the A1, it will be plain sailing," Hans mumbled, trying to unclench his teeth. As he got out to fill the tank, he suggested I head for the little store to buy some munchies for the road. Why should we do that, I wondered, when the airport was only an hour's drive away? I stayed put. So Hans was not only stressed but hungry as he carefully merged onto the highway and slowly headed north. Then we stopped altogether. The gigantic trucks that stream across Europe stopped, the tiny Fiats and Ferraris stopped, the motorbikes stopped, and all the cars crammed with families heading home for the holidays stopped.

We did not move again for the next eighteen hours. Nothing, *niente*, not an inch.

The continuous concrete barriers down the middle of the highway prevented us from trying a U-turn to reach the mysteriously clear lanes heading south. Luckily, we had a full tank of gas, which meant we could run the engine on and off to keep warm. I rummaged around and found a half-full bottle of water under the seat, which we rationed. When this was gone, I filled the bottle with snow and warmed it between my thighs. Not as straightforward as it sounds, with the occupants of the surrounding vehicles using the area as a communal toilet. The revolting images are forever in my head, but I'll leave that scene to your imagination.

As the radio spewed out updates, it became clear we were going to be stuck for a long time. According to the news, this was the worst traffic jam in Italian history, with thousands of vehicles immobilized from Rome to Florence. Not a police car in sight.

Hans eventually dozed off—he can sleep anywhere. Deciding to get comfy, I opened a suitcase and pulled out my pyjamas and a woolly sweater and struggled into them, trying not to flash the truck drivers.

The air ached with cold. The thickening darkness glittered with snowflakes, occasionally lit by headlights as our neighbours turned their engines on and off. It felt like being inside a snow globe, eerie yet strangely beautiful. Then, as I tried to fall asleep, the antics inside a small car in front of us caught my attention. Two people seemed to be wrestling. Oh, yes, right. These two amorous souls were so athletic they were worthy of an Olympic medal. Impressed, even slightly envious, I remained captivated until their windows fogged up and I couldn't see any more. Minutes later, the driver's door opened, and an arm shot out and plonked an open bottle of bubbly into the snow.

The door shut, and I could not take my eyes off that bottle. When I was sure the exhausted couple inside the car, poor things, had fallen asleep, I quietly opened my own door and crept towards the prize. Please don't judge me. In similar circumstances, you would have done the same. I poured a quarter of the Prosecco (well, maybe half), into my empty water bottle. It was the best drink I have ever had and, no, I did not share a drop with my sleeping partner.

Around noon the next day, the engines of the surrounding cars came to life. And then Hans turned the key in our own ignition and, inch by inch, we moved north, crawling slowly past jack-knifed trucks and broken-down and abandoned vehicles. By the time we made it to the Florence airport, we found that it had closed for the unforeseeable future. We drove on to Pisa, on the Tuscan coast, where the airport was also shut. Ditto Bologna. Travel chaos ruled across Europe; even the flight our sons were taking from Montreal to London was cancelled. In despair, we headed north-west to Parma, the city famous for its cured ham, of little interest to either Hans or me at that moment. Parma airport was also dark. It was so late by then that we slept in the parking lot.

I was awakened by a frantic tapping on the car window. I opened my eyes to find myself face to face with a filthy, bearded vagabond, who was gesturing wildly. Terrified, I tried to scream, but my lips were glued shut (it had been days since I'd used a toothbrush).

It was Hans.

"The airport is open! Flights are departing—we need to run!" he yelled.

In stained and crumpled clothes, with my hair knotted and my eye makeup smudged, I was more than ready to get out of this rental car. We dumped it with a scribbled note to Avis and dragged our luggage to the check-in, where we joined a crowd of travellers who resembled the walking dead. It looked like all of us had slept in our cars. I remember the disbelieving face of the clean, sweet-smelling young woman working the counter as she tried to smile at us. But she had good news: there was a flight to London in forty minutes and we were all on it. In awed and grateful silence, we shuffled two by two onto the plane—our Noah's ark. It turned out the plane was the first to leave Italy in over two days, and among the first in Europe to fly again after the blizzard.


This winter in Tuscany there have been no freak snowstorms so far. The weather is still unseasonably warm. From my cupboard office, I can hear the stonemasons at work on the new retaining wall. And then, like clockwork, they stop their bashing. Soon, the mouth-watering smell of grilled sausages fills the air. I can't help myself. I shut down my laptop and head out the kitchen door to find the men on the terrace, rhapsodizing over today's lunch: along with the sausages, there are marinated red peppers, a salad drenched in last fall's olive oil, slices of local pecorino cheese and bowls of plump and spicy Sicilian olives. The strings of thick sausages spit and hiss on a makeshift barbecue they've constructed from a metal wheelbarrow. They've also set up a long trestle table and covered it with a red-and-white-checked tablecloth.

Claudio, the rounder of the two stonemasons, is carefully polishing a set of wineglasses, holding each one up to the sun for inspection. When he sees me, he gestures to the table. I call Hans and we join them, as do Leonardo, the plumber, who always seems to be here fixing something, and Marcello, the electrician, who rarely leaves the property because there's always wiring to repair. The complexity of our electrical and plumbing systems could rival the International Space Station.

The scene takes me right back to our five years of renovation, when, each working day, everything stopped for the Italian ritual of a "proper" lunch, or *pranzo*, followed by a short nap, and then back to work until the sun set. Hans and I aren't always invited to join the *ragazzi*, but today they're in a celebratory mood; there is a long weekend of festivities ahead, yet another saint's day. Marcello has brought his homemade brew, a giant bottle of rough, label-less wine. Proudly, he pours the blackcurrant-coloured liquid into the sparkling wineglasses. The first sip is ferocious, but with each bite of the hearty food, his wine becomes quite drinkable. An afternoon nap is inevitable.

> "I'd much rather eat pasta and
> drink wine than be a size zero."
> —SOPHIA LOREN

# "Don't Worry, They Won't Die"

Winter is the prime season for comfort food, those yummy, warm, calorific dishes that pull at our heartstrings and live forever in our memories. Whether it's tucking into macaroni and cheese after a disappointing day or sharing bowls of homemade chicken soup with your mum after school, comfort food can also be a way of saying sorry or I love you.

In Britain, the ultimate wintery homecooked meal would be a no-fuss shepherd's pie, sometimes known as cottage pie. The classic recipe calls for a mashed potato topping over a filling of carrots, onions and minced meat, usually lamb. My mother made it often, not only because it was an inexpensive dish that stretched a long way, but also because everyone else in our large family loved it. Except me. I could manage a few bites if I scraped every morsel of mashed potato off the top. If even a slither touched my lips, I would gag (blame it on the nuns, a story for later). And things only got worse when I was badly traumatized by a shepherd's pie.

When my father died at thirty-nine, tragically young, he left us with little except for our house. It was hardly a palace, but it did have five bedrooms (two of them the size of a closet) and two bathrooms, unheard of in our parts, where most working-class folks lived in compact Victorian row houses, with the privy, as it was known, in a tiny shed at the bottom of the garden. Though the house was fully paid off, I grew up watching my widowed mother counting every penny. Monday to Friday she took in lodgers— managers at the local light bulb factory who would live with us during the working week, then return to London, and their own families, for the weekend. We usually had three guests, always men, each with their own bedroom, which meant my mother, my three siblings and I had to squish up in the remaining two. In return for their rent, my mother kept their rooms tidy, did their laundry and prepared a full English breakfast of eggs, bacon and fried tomatoes each morning and their supper every evening. By the end of the week, money was always tight, and she had to get creative when it came to cutting corners.

One day I arrived home from school to find her in her usual position at the kitchen stove, frying onions. That is always a tantalizing smell.

"Mmmm, what are you cooking?"

"A shepherd's pie for the lodgers," my mother said.

I noticed two empty dog food cans on the counter. We did not have a dog.

Seeing the shock on my thirteen-year-old face, she said, "Oh, pull yourself together. With plenty of onions, some peas and carrots, and loads of Worcestershire sauce, they'll never know the difference."

"Never know the difference!" I bellowed. "You are going to poison the lodgers and go to jail."

"It's fine for dogs, so don't worry, they won't die," she retorted, turning back to the frying pan. "Go do your homework."

I spent the lodgers' suppertime sitting at the bottom of the stairs, fixated on the closed dining room door, behind which the men were tucking into dog food. Then the door opened and Patrick, my favourite of the three men, smiled at me and said, "That shepherd's pie was exceptional. Would you ask your mother if there's enough for seconds?"

My mother was right. They didn't die.


Maybe one reason I've always felt so contented in Italy is simply the pasta. To me, pasta, in all its wondrous varieties, is the ultimate comfort food. Tuck into a bowl of fettuccini Alfredo, spaghetti alle vongole, macaroni and cheese, or gnocchi smothered in a buttery sage sauce, and immediately the world seems a friendlier place and my problems dissolve. Sure, they come back, but for the moment, all I can concentrate on is eating the pasta and enjoying life.

Pasta is an important part of the women's retreats we run here—both eating it and learning how to make it from scratch. Gathered around the giant stone island in the kitchen, we each crack an egg into our pile of flour, stir up the dough, roll it out and then rub, twist and pull it into a variety of shapes. Putting twenty strangers together in a kitchen to make pasta and drink wine is inevitably a recipe for new friendships.

When we opened our doors in 2015, I simply wanted to share the joys of Tuscany with groups of women taking a time-out from their regular lives to experience a rare camaraderie in this magical place. During these retreats, women talk from morning lattes until the last glass of wine at night. So often, their emotions are raw. As it turned out, while women do come to the villa to celebrate successes in life, thanks to being in the right place at the right time, hard work and perseverance, many also bring along their heart-breaks, disappointments and grief. Gathering these groups to do what we do best here—talking and having fun—really does help mend hearts, alleviate fear and ignite ideas for the future.

On the final evening of each retreat, we celebrate with lasagna—what else! Not only is it the ultimate Italian comfort food, but the lasagna we serve is the best, created by Maria, the pasta queen, who lives up the hill in the medieval village of Montefollonico. Our village has a taverna, a pharmacy and, most essential, an *alimentari*, or grocery store, that sells just about everything. Need a blackboard? They'll have it. Under the cheese counter, they stock the odd hammer and screwdriver. If you want to catch up on juicy local gossip and ominous weather predictions, drop in when the farmers are picking up their daily panini lunches.

Maria is the store's proprietor, working alongside her two grown daughters, Natalie and Guila. They all keep a kind and watchful eye on the well-being of the villagers, especially the elderly, of whom there are many. They help book doctors' appointments, they organize school pickups and, given that there aren't any takeout restaurants in Tuscany, Maria and her daughters offer a freshly made dish of the day. Thursday is lasagna day. At the crack of dawn, a pilgrimage of working mothers, teens on their way to school and the usual octogenarians place their empty casserole dishes in a box at the front of the store. On the way home later in the day, they pick up piping-hot, decadent, creamy and absolutely perfect lasagna. During the Covid pandemic, these women were a lifeline, especially for the village's elderly.

And now I've persuaded Maria to share her lasagna recipe to comfort us all.

# LASAGNA

### SERVES 6 TO 8

*Lasagna is one of the best-known and oldest pasta dishes. The flat sheets of pasta go as far back as ancient Rome, but the first reference to lasagna itself is in a fourteenth-century English cookbook. Each region of Italy seems to have a different style of lasagna, and the ladies who run the village shop have their own special recipe, beloved by the residents of Montefollonico.*

*This vegetarian version is as cozy as a blanket on a wintry day. It can also be a summer crowd-pleaser, served with a crisp green salad on the side.*

### Pasta Sheets:
1½ cups 00 flour (unbleached all-purpose also works)

3 large eggs

1 tablespoon extra virgin olive oil

### Veggie Sauce:
2 tablespoons extra virgin olive oil

1 large onion, diced

1 clove garlic, thinly sliced

1 large zucchini, thinly sliced

10 ounces (300 g) mushrooms, chopped

Salt and freshly ground black pepper

½ cup heavy cream

1 small glass white wine

*continued...*

*Béchamel:*

½ cup butter

½ cup all-purpose flour

4 cups whole milk (2% will also do)

Salt and freshly ground black pepper

1 cup freshly grated Parmesan cheese

*To make the pasta sheets:* Pile the flour onto a clean surface and make a well in the centre. Add the eggs and mix gently with a fork. Add the olive oil and knead for 8 to 10 minutes, adding a little more flour if needed. The dough should become smooth and compact. Roll the dough into a ball and cover with clear plastic wrap. Refrigerate for 30 minutes.

Using a pasta machine or a rolling pin, roll out the dough into almost translucent sheets, 12 inches (30 cm) long. With a sharp knife, cut the sheets into strips about 2¾ inches (7 cm) wide, and place them in a single layer on a baking sheet lined with parchment paper. Cover with another sheet of parchment paper to prevent them from drying out until you're ready to cook them.

*To make the veggie sauce:* In a frying pan over medium heat, warm the olive oil (do not let it smoke). Add the onion and garlic and cook, stirring, until browned. Add the zucchini and mushrooms and sauté for about 5 minutes, until the vegetables are soft. Season to taste with salt and pepper. Reduce the heat to low and add the cream. Cook for few minutes, then stir in the wine. Remove from the heat.

*To make the béchamel:* In a medium saucepan, melt the butter over low heat. Gradually add the flour, whisking constantly until the mixture becomes smooth. Gradually add the milk, whisking constantly until the mixture thickens to a smooth sauce. Season to taste with salt and pepper and remove from the heat.

*To assemble the lasagna:* Preheat the oven to 400°F (200°C).

In a large pot of boiling water, cook the fresh lasagna sheets, in batches of two, for 30 seconds per batch. Remove with a slotted spoon and gently place in a colander. Run them under cold water to cool, then lay out on parchment paper.

Lightly oil the bottom of a large casserole dish. Cover with a layer of pasta sheets. Add about a fifth of the veggie sauce, spreading it out evenly over the pasta sheets. Spread on about a fifth of the béchamel. Repeat the layers of pasta, veggie sauce and béchamel, making four more layers, then sprinkle the top with the Parmesan.

Bake for 35 to 40 minutes or until it's bubbling and golden brown on the top.

"The storm starts when the drops start dropping.
When the drops stop dropping then the storm starts stopping."

—DR. SEUSS

# Hold On to Your Hats

Just as I'm hoping winter has forgotten us this year, the temperature drops dramatically. On the morning I usually make my weekly trip to the open market in Montepulciano, I wake up with a sense of doom that deepens when the stonemasons fail to turn up for work.

The last thing I want to do is wander through the market in the cold, but I bundle up and get into my old Defender. Even though I get there long before the usual closing time, some of the stand owners are already packing up their wares. The friendly Afghan who sells pots and pans (and something out of the back of his van that the local teenagers find interesting) is blue-lipped and wearing three layers of puffy jackets. The butcher is loudly complaining to anyone who will stop to listen about the possibility of frostbitten extremities. The proprietor of my favourite cheese stand, usually piled with plump rounds of pecorino, is loading up his truck. He growls through chattering teeth, "The winds are coming."

He is right.

Italian winds are not for the faint of heart. Nicknamed "the boot" for the shape it makes, Italy is surrounded by seas: the Mediterranean in the west, the Adriatic in the east and the Tyrrhenian and Ionian in the south. Then there are the mountains. To the north, the Alps, and, running down the centre of the country, the Apennines, a craggy spine that splits much of Italy in half. Across the water from Sicily, at the tip of the boot, is the African continent. I am by no means a meteorologist, but I was fascinated by geography at school. So bear with me for a moment while I indulge my inner weatherwoman.

Because of the extreme differences in climate from the freezing Alps to the scorching deserts of North Africa, the winds here can be ruthless, and the Italians have named them all. The Sirocco comes from the south, carrying red sand from the Sahara that annoyingly coats everything around the villa. Then, in early fall, there is the Levante, an easterly wet wind that seems to come out of nowhere, soaking us. Every summer I long for the Ponente, a delicious westerly breeze that brings relief during the intense heat. But the one I dread most is the bone-chilling winter wind, the Tramontana, which hurtles across the snow-packed Alps and storms down to Tuscany, sending everyone running for cover and bolting their shutters tight. I was brought up in the wettest part of Europe, the county of Lancashire, so I'm a veteran of interminable sleeting rain. But nothing had prepared me for the drama of the Tramontana.

As I rush back from the market, the wind pummels my old but sturdy vehicle from both sides. Ahead of me, a tiny Fiat 500 is shunted into the roadside ditch as if flicked by a giant's finger. The driver waves to say she is fine, even though both she and her car are upside down. I think about stopping and am relieved to see a couple of guys pull over and run to help.

Battling on, I finally turn up the driveway to find Hans waiting nervously for me under dancing cypress trees. The gale is so strong now it bends them into a full curtsy, then whiplashes them upright with such force it seems amazing they don't snap. We flee inside, trying not to panic, which is frankly impossible with the wind howling like a pack of wolves down the narrow gorge on one side of the villa. The electrics hiss and flash, on and off, on and off, until we splutter into darkness. We light candles to a continuous banging— rattle thump, rattle thump—as the wind slaps the outside shutters against the stone walls. We hear the menacing sound of wood split- ting, followed by a ferocious screaming that reverberates around us as the Tramontana tears the shutters from their hinges. We watch from the safety of our bedroom as all eight shutters on the east side of the villa fly across the valley, followed by five newly planted olive trees and my favourite wooden bench, never to be found.

The storm rages for two days. By the third, its bite has loosened, but the relentless rain has me searching for flights to somewhere warm, somewhere cheap, somewhere nearby, but with sunshine. Perugia airport is only forty minutes away. A small converted army base, not much bigger than a car dealership, it's home to several discount airlines that fly to a handful of destinations. I soon spot a cheap flight to Trapani, not far from the stunning city of Palermo in Sicily. The temperature there is a delectable 26°C (79°F). To top it off, tomorrow is Valentine's Day. Hans and I can have a romantic adventure!

"Oh my gawd, Hans, there is a flight for only ten euros to Palermo! Come on, whisk me away to blue skies." There may be a slightly unappealing whine in my voice.

It takes him a while to respond, but finally my Romeo announces, "I've looked at the flight and the price has gone up."

"No," I wail with bitter disappointment.

"It's now eighteen euros," he says, and goes back to whatever important task he is doing.

"I'll go alone!"

No response this time.

Is he joking? Sadly, no. I try to be understanding about my Valentine's reluctance. It's true that we face days of cleanup from the winds, the least of which is replacing the shutters it tossed across the valley.

But after a few hours of wifely glaring—and the constant muttering of "The tickets are the price of a coffee and sandwich! Couldn't we at least go for the day?"—the tickets are booked.

The next morning, we are on our way to Sicily for lunch! No luggage, no laptops, free as the wind. At the airport, we park the car and breeze past passport control and straight onto the plane.

We arrive in what feels like another country. In a holiday mood, we rent a convertible at the Trapani airport and meander through picturesque orchards of ripening blood oranges on the short journey to Palermo. Then, as we quite often do, we take a wrong turn and find ourselves on a dirt road, surrounded by a shepherd and his flock of sheep, an Instagram moment calling to be captured. I grab my phone. Before I have time to click the biblical scene, a huge Maremma sheepdog is trying to climb through the open top of the car. These dogs may look like cuddly polar bears, but they can be vicious when protecting their flock. As the dog attempts to chew through the rolled-back canvas roof, the shepherd wanders over and proceeds to bash the car with a large stick. We're unsure whether this is to get rid of the dog, which does work, or to take out his anger on the tourists who are in the way of his sheep. After he demolishes the paintwork down one side of the rental car, the dog flees and we roar off, scattering the flock in every direction.

Not thrilled at the state of the car and what this inexpensive one-day trip is now going to cost, Hans drives on to Palermo, where chaos greets us. Vehicles are perilously parked wherever their owners fancied leaving them. When we finally manage to squeeze our battered convertible between some overflowing garbage bins and an open truck loaded down with firewood, we hop out—and into the path of a donkey laden with massive bags of red onions. Everyone around us is shouting at someone else in a dialect we barely understand. Still, the fumes of gasoline mixed with the intense sweetness emanating from street carts piled with mountains of fried doughnuts are intoxicating. We are definitely in another world.

We enter the walled city, in all its faded splendour, through one of several medieval gates—which has been expensively restored after being badly damaged in the Second World War, or so the plaque tells us—and push our way through the crowds into the old town, the *centro*. Its narrow streets are lined with handcarts and trestle tables toppling with vegetables we won't see in Tuscany for at least another month: green beans a yard long hanging from washing lines, wild asparagus as thin as pencils, mounds of turnip greens, rainbows of peppers and piles of glossy eggplants, all being bartered over by boisterous shoppers. Then, from behind a pyramid of yellow-skinned winter melons, an unshaven Sicilian with a paunch as rotund as his wares beckons. Picking a melon from the mound of cannonballs, he splits it open and passes us a slice of white, juicy deliciousness to taste. Licking our lips, we thank him, the sweetness energizing us enough to keep pushing through the crowd.

Finally, we find our way out of bedlam and into Palermo's old port, La Cala, which for charm rivals any picturesque harbour anywhere. Multicoloured fishing boats bob alongside fancy yachts from as far away as Hamburg and Houston. I have at last won my husband over. We stroll along hand in hand, remembering once more why we love Italy, until it's time for lunch.

We pick a restaurant on the edge of the water with tables covered in blue-and-white cloths. There is only one option on the menu. Plonking down a jug of chilled rosé wine and a bowl of olives, the waitress, whose unruly corkscrew curls are as black as the olives and whose eyes are that Sicilian sapphire, explains the day's meal to us: caponata, followed by grilled fish, caught that morning, and granita for dessert, all made by her mama and her *nonna*. Who can argue?

I've never tasted caponata before. When she delivers ours, I emulate the surrounding diners and scoop a mouthful onto warm toast. I die and go to foodie heaven. The closest dish I've eaten is ratatouille, a French eggplant stew that Brits usually manage to turn wet, soggy and tasteless. The Sicilian version is in a class of its own, a small jar brimming with a glossy, colourful mix of cooked eggplant, peppers, olives and tiny capers. It's sublime: not too oily, not too vinegary, both sweet and sour, like a thick, coarse relish. Even saying the word out loud as I type it—*ka-puh-naa-tuh*—is a thrill.

The rest of the lunch is just as delicious.

Somehow, we manage to get ourselves and our full stomachs back to the airport. A day in Sicily is just what we needed to recharge our batteries, and an excellent way to spend Valentine's Day.

# CAPONATA

SERVES 6

*There are as many versions of caponata, a chunky, savoury-sweet-sour Sicilian stew of glistening goodness, as there are southern Italian kitchens, but this one is based on the one we first ate in Palermo. It's taken me a while to perfect my own, but I think it's just as mouth-watering.*

*Traditionally, this is a summer dish, but I make it all year, as an accompaniment to grilled fish or meat, or even a baked potato. Caponata can also be a meal all by itself. My favourite lunch is a large dollop served on French bread with a slice of creamy Camembert on top.*

*The key to the perfect caponata is the depth of flavour of the briny olives, capers, wine vinegar and raisins added to a chunky mix of vegetables, the basis of which is eggplant.*

*Make a big batch, as it will last about six weeks in the fridge.*

2 large round eggplants or 3 small long eggplants,
    cut into 1-inch (2.5 cm) cubes

Salt

½ cup extra virgin olive oil

6 ripe tomatoes, diced

2 large red onions, thinly sliced

2 celery stalks, sliced into ½-inch (1 cm) pieces

1 red bell pepper, cut into ½-inch (1 cm) pieces

Freshly ground black pepper

2 tablespoons pitted green, black or mixed olives

2 tablespoons capers in vinegar, rinsed

2 tablespoons red wine vinegar

1 tablespoon sultana raisins

1½ teaspoons granulated sugar
1 teaspoon dried chili flakes
Chopped fresh parsley and/or basil

Place the chunks of eggplant in a colander, sprinkle generously with salt and let stand for about 30 minutes. (This removes the bitterness.) Rinse off the salt and pat dry.

In a frying pan over medium heat, warm the olive oil (do not let it smoke). Add the eggplant and cook, stirring frequently, until golden brown. Using a slotted spoon, transfer the eggplant to a bowl and set aside.

To the same pan, still over medium heat, add a glug more oil. Add the tomatoes, onions, celery and red pepper. Reduce the heat to low and simmer for about 15 minutes, until the vegetables thicken. Season to taste with salt and pepper.

Stir in the olives, capers, vinegar, raisins, sugar and chili flakes and bring to a boil. Return the browned eggplant to the pan, reduce the heat and simmer for 5 to 10 minutes, adding more salt and pepper to taste.

Remove from the heat and let stand for a couple of hours at room temperature, so the flavours infuse. Serve sprinkled with chopped parsley or basil, or a mixture of both.

"A woman is like an artichoke: you must
work hard to get to her heart."
—INSPECTOR JACQUES CLOUSEAU,
*The Pink Panther*

# One Dangerous Artichoke

The Italian for artichoke, *carciofi*, sounds so much like a sneeze it always makes me laugh. *Carciofi* . . . Bless you!

From November through March, you see artichokes everywhere in Tuscany—in vegetable gardens, piled up in markets and even growing along the edge of country roads. I find the plant itself too large, ugly and unruly (like some of my premarital boyfriends). There's no way to ignore them—the rough silvery stalks spread all over, some of them reaching a metre high. Yet right in the middle of all that ungainliness is a striking purple thistle, the bud of which is the culinary delicacy we call an artichoke.

The many varieties create a festival of colour across the market stands from winter into early spring. There is the eye-catching Violetto, small, purple and more elongated than round. Steamed, braised or baked, they are cut lengthwise and served with a dollop of butter and ground pepper. Finger food for the gods.

Then there are artichokes as small as golf balls, tender and sweet, that Italians eat raw. A favourite at Easter, when they are sliced into delicate slivers then drizzled in extra virgin olive oil, sprinkled with salt and pepper, given a squeeze of lemon and topped with shaved Parmigiana-Reggiano.

The most common variety in Italy is the big, round Roman artichoke, or Mammola, which is served stuffed, sautéed or baked, or is chopped and added to risotto and pasta sauces.

The Globe artichoke, as big as a fist, is the one you will find in most supermarkets outside of Italy. It's the first artichoke I ever met, at a nightclub in London. I may be the only person almost killed by an artichoke.

At the time, I was an eighteen-year-old model living in the big city. Like all my model peers, I was always hungry, partly due to a lack of money to spend on food—we spent the little cash we had on party clothes—but also because we were on perpetual starvation diets to "look good" for the camera.

One evening, dressed to make an eighties fashion statement, with all its glitter and glam—boob tube under a shoulder-padded sequined jacket, pencil skirt and black fishnet stockings—I headed for the legendary private member's club Tramp, in Mayfair. On any given night, guests at this infamous honeypot included rockers such as Mick, Rod and Bowie. On the dance floor, you would spot supermodels Iman, Jerry Hall, Brooke and Yasmin Le Bon bopping with the likes of Joan and Jackie Collins, Liza Minnelli, Michael Caine, Jack Nicholson and Danny DeVito. The royals were regulars too. The co-owner, Johnny Gold, promised a space where there would be no gossip columnists and no paparazzi—the only people he out-and-out banned. He didn't even seem to mind members who were unscrupulous businessmen or notorious gangsters—all part of the human circus he was running. For wide-eyed aspiring models like me, it became our stomping ground, a place to hang out with fashion photographers and agents, wangle free cocktails and dance until the early hours.

On the night of the deadly artichoke, I was among a crowd of models, wannabe actresses and some hopeful men invited for dinner at the restaurant adjacent to the dance floor, a favourite of Shirley MacLaine's; the actress could often be found there, tucking into a plate of sausage and mash. The bloke who had invited us, a city banker type, sat at the head of our long table and ordered a meal for all of us. As we waited for the food, I was the only one of the women who wasn't asked to dance. While my friends strutted to Michael Jackson and Tina Turner, I sat uncomfortably alone.

The first course arrived before they got back. The waiter placed three dishes in front of me. One was a small bowl filled with water and a floating slice of lemon; another small bowl contained vinaigrette; and the third was a dinner plate on which rested, all on its own, a warm petalled globe of some kind of vegetable. It was nearly midnight, and I was hungry. Before you continue reading, remember that I grew up in Lancashire, where the cuisine was simple:

fish and chips, meat pies and overly boiled vegetables. I cut up what I now know was a Globe artichoke and slowly crunched through all its leaves, thorns and bristly bits, bite by chewy bite. Since it was scratchy and hard to swallow, I washed it down with the warm water and lemon (from the first finger bowl I'd ever encountered).

Just as I'd cleaned my plate, the others returned, gleaming, from the dance floor. I watched in confusion as they elegantly pulled each leaf from its globe and dipped the soft end in the vinaigrette, stopping every now and then to rinse their fingers in the lemon and water.

When the model sitting next to me asked me where my artichoke was, I told her I had finished it.

"All of it?" she asked, aghast.

I was just about to say I didn't feel well when a dribble of blood escaped the corner of my mouth.

My friends pulled me to my feet, half carried me out of the club and hailed me a cab to the nearest hospital ER. Apart from a damaged ego and a throat that stayed sore for a few days, I was fine. Except for a deathly fear of artichokes.

I would have scoffed to hear that the ancient Greeks and Romans believed that artichokes had therapeutic powers. Even so, it took hundreds of years for the thistly things to become a sought-after delicacy—until the fifteenth century, when the mega-rich Florentine Medici family began to feast on them. Now this highly nutritious vegetable is enjoyed by all, including me. Among the many benefits of living in Tuscany is that I have finally conquered my fear of the artichoke.

# ARTICHOKES

*A friend once told me she adored the taste of artichokes but was put off cooking them as they seemed like way too much work. She is both right and wrong. While I have made artichoke pasta sauces that have left me screaming "Never again!" it would be a shame to pass up on the wonders of this unique vegetable, packed with nutrients. Buried beneath the tough outer leaves is a tender, buttery treasure: the heart of the artichoke. Here are two very easy recipes, one using canned or jarred artichoke hearts; the other, cooked.*

## Creamy Artichoke Dip

MAKES ABOUT 2 CUPS

*This is a delicious and easy-to-make dip that can be used as a topping on crostini or served with crudités and crackers as a pre-dinner nibble. It pairs perfectly with a glass of crisp rosé.*

1 can (14 oz/398 ml) artichoke hearts in brine or water
1 clove garlic, grated or finely minced
½ cup fresh ricotta
4 tablespoons freshly grated Parmesan cheese
2 tablespoons chopped fresh basil
1 to 2 tablespoons extra virgin olive oil
1 tablespoon freshly squeezed lemon juice
Salt and freshly ground black pepper

Drain the artichoke hearts and add them to a food processor fitted with a steel blade. Add the garlic, ricotta, Parmesan, basil, 1 tablespoon of the olive oil and the lemon juice. Process until the dip is smooth but not runny. If it's too lumpy, add a little more olive oil. Season to taste with salt and pepper, and give it another quick whiz.

NOTE: Alternatively, you can add all the ingredients to a large bowl and mix with a hand blender.

# Artichoke Tart

### SERVES 4

*I prefer fresh artichokes in this recipe, for their superior flavour and texture, but you can use well-drained jarred or canned artichoke hearts instead. This tart is delightful served hot, warm or cold, with a crisp salad of lettuce and tomatoes on the side.*

6 whole artichokes, well scrubbed
4 tablespoons extra virgin olive oil
1 large onion, chopped
1 teaspoon brown sugar
1 teaspoon balsamic vinegar
4 large eggs
⅓ cup heavy or whipping cream
2 teaspoons each chopped fresh parsley, sage and oregano
Salt and freshly ground black pepper
½ cup crumbled full-fat soft goat cheese
½ cup finely grated Parmesan cheese
1 package (14 oz/400 g) frozen puff pastry, thawed

*continued...*

Preheat the oven to 400°F (200°C).

Bring a large pot of water to a boil and add the artichokes. Reduce the heat and simmer for about 30 minutes or until a fork easily pierces an artichoke to the heart. Drain and let stand. Once the artichokes are cool enough to handle, remove the leaves to reveal the hearts. Discard the leaves and cut each artichoke heart into quarters.

In a frying pan over medium heat, warm the olive oil. Add the onion and sauté for 5 minutes. Add the sugar and vinegar and cook, stirring occasionally, until the onions are crispy and golden. Remove the onion mixture from the pan and set aside.

In a large bowl, whisk the eggs, setting a little of the whisked egg aside to brush the edge of the pastry later. Stir in the cream and chopped herbs, then season with salt and pepper. Stir in the artichoke hearts, onion mixture, goat cheese and Parmesan.

Roll out the pastry and lay it in a 9-inch (23 cm) pie plate. Add the filling, then trim the pastry to fit. Brush the edges with the reserved whisked egg.

Bake for 40 to 45 minutes or until the pastry turns golden. Take it out of the oven and let it cool slightly before serving.

"Life is not measured by time. It is measured by moments."

—ARMIN HOUMAN

# Squeezing Lemons in Winter

It is mating season. The clubs and discos of London in the eighties have nothing on the noise that wakes us in the early hours. The screams of foxes cut through the woods below and echo up to our windows as vixens yowl their whereabouts to the males.

Then there are the deer, who make a mating call resembling a breathless bark. Our guests often ask if there are dogs in the woods, and I tell them, "Only in the fall hunting season." When I explain that the deer are rutting and that for some reason mating Tuscan deer bark, they look at me with "poor crazy lady" raised eyebrows. Apparently, North American deer do not bark. Well, here they do, very loudly and at four in the morning. It's party central in the woods below us.

The birds are also at it. As the males defend their territories, the dawn chorus takes on an aggressive pitch. Nesting season has begun.

When we were restoring the main property, we tossed out the old windows and ripped out the insides of each room. With the windows gone, the swifts ventured inside and built their nests amongst the chestnut beams. Inevitably, as the work progressed, new windows were installed. I arrived home one day to heartbreaking cries of panic as the birds hit the new glass, unable to reach their nests. The ruthless builders didn't care, but I tried to rescue a few nests, some filled with eggs and some with hatched chicks. I lay them gently outside. Futile, of course—they all perished.

As February tumbles into March, sporadic hours of warm sunshine tease me into jumping into pruning, propagating and planting. Donning old overalls from my *Painted House* days (yup, I kept them, a little snugger now but still splattered with paint), I wander around the gardens, wondering where to start, trailed by Massi, the chief gardener. A handsome man, slightly built but sinewy and as strong as an ox, Massi keeps muttering, "*Piano, piano*"—take it slow.

He is right to try to rein in my enthusiasm, of course, because there is nothing more damaging to a garden than an impatient gardener. When I lived in Montreal, I knew I had to wait for the May 21 long weekend for it to be warm enough to plant, leaping into action with all the other garden lovers to elbow my way through the crowds mobbing the local nurseries. In Italy, we are lucky to be gifted with a much earlier and longer spring, but there isn't really a day on the calendar to act as the signal. This year, though, we had an unusually warm February, so I decide to ignore Massi and plant an entire bed of carrot seeds.

Of course, as soon as they sprout, freezing temperatures return and every single one of them is frosted to death. I don't know the Italian for "I told you so" (after ten years here, I am shamefully still not the least bit fluent), but that doesn't matter—Massi's expression says it all.

And he doesn't even mention the lesson I should have learned from our lemon trees. From Sicily north to Rome, lemon trees thrive planted in the ground, but farther north they must live in large terracotta pots.

The tradition of potting lemon trees began in the formal gardens of the magnificent villas of Florence, Siena and around the great lakes of Como and Garda. I have twenty-five potted lemon trees that are able to survive the winter only if we load each one onto a wheelbarrow before it gets frosty and drag it into a specially built glass house known as a *limonaia*. There they bloom all winter, scenting the air with their tiny white flowers. I don't mind the extra labour—they are beautiful, of course, but they also supply us with an abundance of fresh lemons throughout the winter months. And this year, when the weather warms up, they will line the perimeter of the new terrace to stop tipsy guests (of which we get quite a few) from tumbling over the edge.

What Massi is forbearing to mention, however, is that last year, I insisted on hauling the lemon trees in their giant pots out of the glass house too early, and the little sods were frost-nipped and did not produce a single lemon for the rest of the summer.

When I told one group of retreat guests there would be no limoncello-making for the lack of lemons, one woman actually burst into tears, saying, "But that is why I came!"

I was kidding—there are always plenty of lemons in the market.

But she was right to look forward to it. Limoncello-making is the happiest of workshops. Screams of delight reverberate around the greenhouse as we mix the ingredients together in giant glass vases: lots of squeezed lemons, cups of granulated sugar, 75 percent grain alcohol diluted with 20 percent vodka, and a little water added to stop the consumer going blind.

The women squeeze, grate, pour and taste to get the delightful concoction just right. We then leave it for a month to ferment, but they get to tuck into a batch made by previous guests.

The problem with limoncello is, it just tastes too good—a silky, lemony, sweet drink hiding the lethal booze within. In Italy, it is a favourite digestif, served as a small after-dinner drink. At Villa Reniella, I see it being poured into large wineglasses and tumblers. It goes down well, but you can guarantee that no one will be up for yoga the following morning.

> "It is only when you see people looking ridiculous
> that you realise just how much you love them."
> —AGATHA CHRISTIE

# Nuns and Mashed Potatoes

It's been a busy morning of answering emails, and I am still in my pyjamas. I wander out onto the new terrace, clutching a cup of coffee. The work is nearly finished. The builders are quite familiar with my eccentric outfits of flowery PJs tucked inside knee-high rubber boots. But they're not around. They've all popped up to the village for lunch to celebrate the end of the wall project, so I'm free to roam naked if I so desire.

The terrace floor has been extended with old stone slabs we bought from an unscrupulous antiques dealer in the countryside outside Rome. He sells a variety of stones that he says have been rescued from a Sicilian piazza about to be demolished. Really? His enormous yard is filled with crates of the slabs, sorted into size and colour and about to be shipped to addresses from California to Saudi Arabia. As to the exorbitant prices, he explains, "Well, they are antiques, and when they're gone, they're gone." Weird, given that he never sells out. I am convinced there are towns all over

Italy with paving stones missing, but they are beautiful and I cannot resist them.

I gaze around, imagining where the furniture will go now that the space has tripled in size and thinking about the art classes and dance parties we can now throw here. But then I stop dead, staring at the base of the wall in horror. This is not right! A two-foot-wide border of wet grey concrete runs around the whole terrace, burying the wiring that will power the lanterns. Where it lies, I had planned to plant a bed of honeysuckle that would climb up the high terrace walls. I cannot plant over bloody concrete. And here I am alone, with no one to shout at—Hans disappeared hours ago on some errand (probably including a sneaky stop at the bakery, seeing as we're dieting again). And the concrete is setting, fast.

There is only one thing for it. Still in my pyjamas and wellies, I grab a spade and a wheelbarrow and begin the dirty task of digging up the wet, sticky mess. I work frantically, wanting to get it out before it dries, and soon I'm splattered from head to foot. Then I hear laughter. Angrily, I squint against the sun and make out three figures backlit in the glare. The stonemasons are back! Just as I'm about to let loose a stream of Italian profanities (I know enough Italian to swear), I hear a familiar voice saying, "Mum, what on earth are you doing?"

All thoughts of murder vanish in an instant. Hans was not out sneaking cream buns, after all. He'd gone to pick up our sons, Josh and Max, from the airport. They've come from London and Toronto, respectively, not only to surprise me with a visit, but also to build potting tables for the greenhouse. A belated Christmas present I had forgotten all about!

Hans calls the builders and, between us all, we dig and scrape away the wet concrete. Topsoil goes down in its place, hiding the wires and ready for the plants. I make a spaghetti lunch for everyone, including the builders, and all is forgiven.

Over the next week, Josh and Max work on building the new potting tables, but word has gotten out that the boys are back in town and the invitations roll in. Each afternoon, they set down their tools and we head out to meet friends and explore as a family.

A Dutch couple who befriended us after we moved here asks us to join them one afternoon to watch the *palio* and go back to their place for a light dinner. You may have heard of the famous *palio* held every year in Siena? It's a race in which gorgeous men dress up in full medieval costume—pure theatre—and ride magnificent horses at breakneck speed around the majestic Piazza del Campo. That is *not* the *palio* our Dutch friends are talking about. They mean the race that takes place in nearby Torrita di Siena, home of numerous derelict brick and terracotta pot factories. The town was once world famous for traditionally made terracotta, or baked earth. Sadly, much of the industry has moved abroad.

It may not be a prosperous town, but it does have the annual Palio dei Somari, held in a large parking lot. Instead of beautiful steeds, this race features a motley collection of donkeys being ridden by enthusiastic locals. Such as Leonardo, our plumber, who, as he loves to remind us, was last year's grand champion. I adore donkeys, and if I had any spare time to look after them, I would love a few on our land. They strike me as noble and hard-working, but it's true that they can be painfully stubborn. Which can add much hilarity to the goings-on at this parking lot *palio*.

As we all find places to watch the race, we spot the first rider prancing about on a skinny black donkey. It's the local tax inspector—no one's favourite. Hoots and whistles greet the arrival of a comical threesome, the jolly baker with his two plump sons, all of them kitted out in shiny green tights, riding three donkeys that seem a little too small for their loads. Then comes the butcher, the one who is missing two fingers after a mishap with a pork chop; from the talk around us, he is apparently the favourite to win.

Our plumber, still pumped up from his previous glory, leads the way to the starting line. The serious-looking riders line up, the pistol pops, and they are off. All but our furious plumber, whose donkey wanders off in the wrong direction to munch on a tasty-looking sage bush. The butcher, as predicted, comes in first, and the crowd goes wild.

Afterwards, we head to our friends' house for supper, as planned. Though, as is the Italian way, the guests have grown in number (around here, the motto is: "Add more pasta and there will be plenty to go around"). We're joined by friends from Atlanta, visiting the area, and two elderly neighbours who've popped in after the smell of what's cooking drifted through their window. Our friends have also invited a couple of cheerful nuns who watched the race near us.

While everyone is happily reliving the afternoon's hilarity—the best bit being when the town's mayor skidded in a pile of steaming donkey poo as he was handing out the trophies, sending all the children, including my own, into fits of laughter—Hans slips a comforting hand into mine. He knows I am not happy. I do not do well around nuns, to the point that I feel chilled and shaky. These two are from the local orphanage, and they are sure, as I keep telling myself, to be loving, kind people. I keep my composure in our friends' kitchen, fighting down my demons. But I'm not composed, even as I write this. I'm a grown-up now, though, so I'm no longer afraid. Instead, I'm sad.

In my childhood, people in Lancashire were not all that rich; it is still a predominantly working-class area. If parents living in these mill towns wanted their children to get a decent education that was affordable, they enrolled them behind the high walls of a convent school, whether they were Catholic or not. As mine did with me. But my convent education came at a price extracted by an order of sisters who believed that discipline in the classroom should be not only forceful but cruel.

Most of us remember something about our first day of school. I certainly remember mine. Leading up to it, I was an over-enthusiastic five-year-old, giddy at the prospect of being the first child in our family to go to school. I recall helping my mother pack my satchel, adding my pencil case, a ruler, a handkerchief and a small lollypop. My father, the sweetest and kindest of men, took time off work to accompany me to the convent; on the first day, a parent could stay with each student as a special treat. Head high in my spanking-new uniform of grey skirt, white polo shirt and navy cardigan, I clutched his strong, rough hand as we walked up the path to the towering front door. Once a private home, the sprawling red-brick Victorian-era building was now part chapel, part working convent and part primary school; the nuns lived, worshipped and taught under this one roof. My dad was allowed to stay with me the whole first day, and that evening, I gushed with stories of my initiation around the supper table. I announced that I loved school.

The nightmare began the following morning, when my mother explained that I had to go back again, not just for another day, but for weeks and years to come. I'd assumed that school was a one-day, once-in-a-lifetime experience, like going to a fun fair. No such luck. My mother, who was far stricter than my dad, had to drag me back to the convent, where she left me, sobbing, with Sister Renata—or Sister Tomato, the nickname the older students had given her because of her round, flushed face.

I sobbed as I followed my calmer fellow pupils, holding hands crocodile-style, into our classroom. I sobbed through early-morning prayers, standing knock-kneed and shaking beside my desk. (Since I wasn't a Catholic, I had no clue as to why I should pray, and would later be punished for this fact, relentlessly.) I sobbed when Sister Tomato thumped me on my scrawny shoulder, demanding that I stop crying, her face truly living up to her nickname. I desperately tried to stop, but it was futile—I was inconsolable (not that anyone tried to console me).

The classroom, once a high-ceilinged bedroom, was vast, with its two massive mahogany wardrobes now storing everything required for children to learn. At the front sat Sister's desk. To the right of it was a closed door. On that second day, Sister opened that door and shoved Cindy, a pretty girl with auburn pigtails, through it for speaking out of turn. I was horrified.

A few days later, it was Suzie (soon my best friend)—sentenced for the crime of giggling whilst Sister was speaking. Most days, in fact, Sister forced at least one terrified victim to serve time behind the door.

Eventually I managed to stop sobbing at school, and I tried my best to stay under Sister's radar by being a good girl and keeping my head down. Then came the morning the nun was prowling the rows of desks as we did our sums and noticed the teddy bear stuffed under my chair. Melodramatically, she banged my desk lid with her fist. Woe betide a five-year-old who needed a comfort toy. I glanced up at her face and realized with utter fear just how livid she was, her bushy black eyebrows drawn together in a fierce scowl. I gulped. My time had come. She marched me up to the front of the classroom, opened the door and shoved me through, then slammed the door behind me.

I found myself in an oversized bathroom. The walls, tiled in institutional green, loomed over me. Every fixture seemed fit for a giant, especially the Victorian cast-iron tub that stood in the middle of the room. To add to the torment, a grid of gurgling pipes roared into life every few minutes, terrifying me.

I cried so hard and for so long I had an accident. Still sniffling, I rinsed my knickers and hung them to dry on the scalding pipes.

It was lunchtime when the door finally opened again— I knew because my stomach was growling with hunger. Sternly, Sister told me to put on my underwear and wash my tear-blotched face in cold water. Before she led me back into the classroom, she hissed through tight lips, "Punishment for bad behaviour is not to be discussed with parents."

I ended up spending a lot of time in that bathroom. I was not alone. Most of the little girls in my class did stints in there, grateful that we were not boys. When the nuns decided that a boy needed discipline—for being naughty or too boisterous or just slow to learn—he was frogmarched to the headmistress, the cruellest of them all, for a caning. That punishment was both brutal and humiliating.

As per Sister Tomato's threat, I never uttered a word to my parents about how many times I was locked in that bathroom. I guess I thought it was part of everyone's school life—as a kid you tend to accept the cards you have been dealt. Then came the day, three years later, when events unfolded that led to me being rescued.

Being locked in the bathroom was horrible, but it had nothing on the lunches at the convent. They were repulsive. The dinner ladies (as they are still called in British schools) were all younger nuns, and many of them were kind to us. But they did not shine in the kitchen, serving us overcooked slop that would have been rejected by prison inmates. In the north of England, *dinner* means lunch and *tea* means dinner. (In the posher south, *lunch* is lunch, *tea* means afternoon tea, and *dinner* is dinner. Confusing, I know.) But the point is that lunch at the convent meant a hot meal, no matter how tasteless.

For some draconian reason, we weren't allowed to drink water during meals, so we had nothing to wash down the boiled turnips, rancid cabbage, tasteless carrots and slices of unknown meat floating in gelatinous gravy. Or the overcooked potatoes, sometimes boiled, occasionally baked, but most often mashed, served with an ice-cream scoop that delivered a tepid blob of grey, lumpy goo onto our plates. My friend Sita and I always sat together at lunch. One of the few Indian kids in the school, she loathed mashed potato as much as I did. I'd had my first taste of aromatic curry and rice at her house, so I knew she had even more reason than I did to dislike the bland glop on our plates.

On the day that led to my rescue, for once a sympathetic server let us both skip the viscous scoop of mash. Delighted, we carried our trays through the dining room, past tables full of pupils aged five to eleven, to our spot, hoping we'd escaped the notice of the teachers, mostly nuns, who all sat at the top table. Especially one tormentor, Sister Beverley, who, with her long, pinched face and cruel eyes, constantly searched for rule breakers. But no—she swiftly realized that the scoop of mash was missing from our meal. Making a beeline for us, she grabbed our plates and returned to the serving station, where she added a double dose of potatoes to each one. As Sita began to sob, I held her hand under the table. I was close to tears too, because Sister was about to make an example of us—the school rules stated that we had to eat everything on our plates because, as the nuns never failed to remind us, there were starving children in Africa who would be thrilled to have this food.

With the entire dining room watching, the nun pushed Sita's face into her plate, smearing her wire-rimmed glasses and splattering her long, glossy black hair with mash. "Eat it," the nun squawked. Sita gagged, spluttered and kept on crying as this "woman of God" shoved potatoes into her mouth. None of the adults intervened—they never did. Paralyzed with fear, I waited my turn. But for some unfathomable reason, Sister Beverley strode back to the teachers' table, and my turn never came. For the rest of lunch, the dining room was silent. Not a single soul wanted to risk becoming the next victim.

That evening, tucked up in bed, I finally told my mother what was going on. As she cradled me, I recounted the lunchtime incident and, starting to sob, soldiered on with stories about being locked in the school bathroom and the general bullying behaviour of the nuns. Mum never said a word, but the next day she arrived early for the school pickup to find I'd again been confined to the bathroom. The image of my outraged mother barging in and marching me out of the school is still fresh in my memory. Even better, I never returned.

Years later, I heard that the nuns were dispatched to other convents or to retirement homes and the school was bulldozed to make way for a new housing development. I don't know about my fellow pupils, but I still live with the scars and the shame of those first years at school, which surface every time I am faced with a nun or a plate of mashed potatoes.


The sun is shining, and the unmistakable smell of spring is in the air. I'm ready to start seeding and propagating in earnest, feeling so grateful for the long wooden benches my sons crafted for the greenhouse. It was only a fleeting visit, but we spent some marvellous family time together. What a joy to watch them chatting and working alongside each other, with not one argument—a miracle—brothers who now live far apart but are still so close.

A week after they surprised me, all spattered in my pyjamas, I hug them goodbye with a full heart. As they shove and tumble into the car, Hans reprimands them as if they're still little boys, which makes me smile. But I, too, find the concept that they're now grown men hard to grasp at times.

I feel sure fate played a key role in the good fortune that resulted in me having this unexpected family. One minute, I was a glam twentysomething, cruising down Chelsea's King's Road without a thought for anyone but myself. A chance meeting at a party in the south of France sent me reeling: a new country, a husband and two babies—all within twenty months. I know that many millennials struggle with anxiety. By anxiety, do they mean the constant panic I felt through those turbulent years?

I know I was in shock at the beginning, for sure. Hans and I met and married within weeks, never having gone on a proper date. What had I done? Suddenly I found myself living in a small apartment in Montreal, with screaming little ones, piles of laundry, no friends, no work, coping with a different culture, barely able to remember my London life. Even though I loved my little family, it took me five years to fit in and make new friends.

Still, I loved being a mother. Most of the time. I admit that, unlike my own mother, who felt she was doing fine if we were fed, clean and dressed and otherwise could look after ourselves, I was a helicopter parent. I never missed a parent-teacher evening at school. I went to all the boys' sports events. I supervised their homework and, as a family, we regularly chatted about their futures (not a subject my own mother ever discussed).

It seems like only yesterday that we dropped them off for the first time at a camp in rural Quebec. (This was an alien concept to me—British children rarely go to summer camp.) I watched in astonishment as the other parents deposited their kids and danced back to their cars, ecstatic that they had the next three weeks to themselves. Not Hans and me. We were beside ourselves with worry and guilt. We rented a room in a local bed and breakfast and spent three days crawling around in the camp undergrowth, tracking the antics of our little boys through binoculars. Would they make friends, eat junk food (not offered at home), break a limb, slice off a chunk of finger? The answer was yes to everything.

On the third day, a camp counsellor came over to our hiding place. He was only seventeen, but he terrified us. Caught red-handed stalking our children, we were marched to the office, where we were both reprimanded and then promised that our kids would have a magical summer. They did.

But I continued to be a hawk hovering over their every decision.

I was happy for Josh when he was accepted at a university in England to study disaster management, but he did not welcome my first response to the news: "Maybe you should start with your bedroom?"

"Not funny, Mum," he growled.

It was my nerves talking. I didn't know how to cope with the fact that both boys were quivering on the edge of the nest, ready to soar away towards their futures.

As I now know, children often come back. I remember a British television series that aired years ago about a couple who were planning exciting adventures now that their four children had moved out and their nest was empty. In the first episode, all the kids came back because of breakups, lost jobs, or just not having enough money to live on their own. The parents rented a studio flat and left the kids the house. The funniest part was that they refused to tell their brood their new address.

Parents sometimes take drastic action to get their children out of the house. Recently in Italy, a seventy-five-year-old mother won a legal battle to evict her two fortysomething sons after she'd repeatedly asked them to live independently. In court she called them *bamboccioni*—big babies.

When both my lads fled their childhood home for university, I felt sad, but not for long. Other mothers bemoaned their quiet houses, but we celebrated the peace and even redecorated, something that had always seemed pointless with two rumbunctious teens around. I was thrilled and relieved they'd moved on to higher education, which I sometimes feel I missed out on. But I did insist on constant updates: "Are you okay? Did you eat? Don't forget to wear a coat."

When my best friend, Jacky, and I were modelling on the other side of the world in Japan, our parents did not seem to worry about us. It was normal in those days to go months without being in touch, though I do remember the two of us lining up at a phone booth in Tokyo to call home. My conversation went something like this:

"Hi, Mum, it's me. I am in Tokyo. Yes, Mum, the one in Japan."

"Are you okay?"

"I am. I've been on four magazine covers and filmed lots of commercials. Yesterday, I was dressed by Nina Ricci for a perfume advertisement. It is incredible here. The Japanese eat raw fish."

"Oh, that's nice. Your brother found an injured bird, and we are feeding it in a shoebox. I've got a pie in the oven. Got to go."

And that was it.

I was a very different mother. When Josh moved into his first university digs, I flew from Montreal to London to settle him in. His room was the size of an average bathroom, which made it challenging for more than two people to be in it at any one time. There was a sink in the corner, but the communal toilet was down the hall, shared by the entire floor. The toilet seat was stuck together with Scotch tape, and the place exuded a smell I will never forget.

In Josh's room, the door to the small wardrobe hung on one hinge. Someone had attempted to paint out the foul graffiti on the walls, but the disgusting stains on the floor beside the bed had me heaving! For his room makeover, I added new cushions, hung curtains and made the bed with lovely linen sheets. The school forbade me to replace the mattress. In fact, the administration had left a brochure lying on the bed for us. Or rather, for *me*. It read something like this:

Dear parent,

Welcome.
We are mindful of your emotions at this precise moment as you scan your precious child's room. We are fully aware how small it is, the stench of stale beer and vomit, the lumpy mattress and the sticky carpet, but please do not waste your time or ours by coming to the admissions office to complain. This is his home for the next year.

Sincerely,
The Administration Office
Kings College London

After I fluffed up the new velvet cushions, Josh said, "This is so cool. Thanks, Mum. You can go now."

—

Each of them made it safely to adulthood. And much as they are still my "boys," they are both married now, with wonderful partners and well-looked-after homes of their own. My job as a parent truly is done—for now, anyway.

I shake myself out of my reverie and wave the lads off.

"Travel safe. See you soon!" I shout after the car.

Then I set off to help Massi and Cristian plant the honey-suckle vines around the new terrace.

# Spring

"Spring is the time of the year when it is summer
in the sun and winter in the shade."
—CHARLES DICKENS

# The To-Do Lists

It is a bright, blue-skied morning. I walk through the olive orchard
that winds behind the villa, tilting my face to the sun to absorb her
energy. The wonder of spring needs no explanation. Wildflowers
seem to have sprouted overnight, blossoms cover the trees, and
bees are gorging on all the splendour. Wild daffodils dot the land,
like spilt yellow paint. I didn't plant them, and I wonder who did.
I consider picking a bunch for the kitchen, but they seem happy
where they are, undisturbed amongst the olive trees.

Spring brings a frenzy of activity. The whole valley and its
*cittadini* and *contadini*—townspeople and farmers—have crawled
out of hibernation, greeting spring with jubilant bedlam. Everyone
is out on the streets, catching up with everyone else—on the price
of food, the arrival of grandchildren, the state of the country—
clustered together, as excited as puppies, tails wagging. Relentless
Tuscan housewives are scrubbing their doorsteps, washing windows
and grooming their front yards. The elderly men are out preparing
their vegetable gardens: raking, weeding and planting. Tables and

chairs have sprouted up outside the cafés, already occupied by those tucking into leisurely conversations over espressos and *cornetti*, a traditional morning pastry. I do think all humans are at their most optimistic, their happiest and friendliest, at the first intimation of spring.

Rain or shine, the new season rushes forward in true March madness, and the work around the villa gains momentum. The first vans loaded up with ladies will arrive at the beginning of May to kick off this year's series of retreats. The new walled terrace is finished, the stonework superb, and with smiles all around, we bid the stonemasons, Claudio and Luca, *alla prossima*. And then we check what comes next on our ever-growing to-do lists.

Yes, I have two of them. The first one lists the reams of annual springtime chores to ready the place for invasion. This is our seventh year running the retreats, not counting the cancelled nightmare Covid year. I'm confident we'll complete the chores we have left to do in time. The second is a wish list, things I would love to do, though I probably won't get to most of them. I'll never travel on the new Orient Express to Venice—far too expensive. I will never learn to ride a motorbike, however much Hans begs, wishing I was able to join him on his biking adventures. I will never make marmalade again; I've tried too many times and it's always a disaster. I will never do another handstand (though I do live in hope). And I will never, ever, buy clothes off Instagram again; each time, the outfits that arrive are unrecognizable from the pictures and would barely fit the most delicate of bodies, of which mine is not. Never say never, they say, but I think with some things it's not so much "never say never" as "know your truth."

There is one item that appears on both lists. Our *piccolo lago*, or small lake (actually more of a pond), has been a white elephant for years—an excruciating mistake in terms of both money and time. And the cause of endless marital spats, as Hans has a habit of reminding me each morning on waking, "If you'd put the damn thing where the natural spring flows, we would not have this problem." Followed by "If you'd only listen."

As I've mentioned, the villa, barn and converted pigsties are perched on top of a steep hill, rather like fingers of toast sticking out of a soft-boiled egg. The area around the buildings is terraced so we don't slide to the bottom of the valley. There are two pieces of flat land, one to the east of us, with a natural spring, and one to the west, with no spring. Tucked away in a corner of my mind when we were renovating this place was the vision of a pond surrounded by reeds and wild irises, a serene spot to hold meditation classes. Since there were more pressing projects presenting themselves, I kept quiet about my watery daydreams, until four years ago, when I spotted a man leaning on the bonnet of a shiny new car he'd parked amongst the trees on a track at the top of the property. Not too unusual in Tuscany—we constantly stumble on vehicles here that belong to wild boar or truffle poachers, or the occasional smooching teens. As I approached, the man greeted me with a movie-star grin. He was dapper, dressed for the office not a country stroll, and even though it was only spring, he had a walnut-coloured tan more suited to the beach.

He thrust a remarkably smooth hand into mine whilst running the other through his sleek black mane. Although he could be nothing but Italian, he addressed me in flawless English, saying, "Good morning. I am Sergio. Are you the proprietor of this magnificent property?"

I told him I was, and he explained that he was a specialist pond builder. Was I, perhaps, interested in such a thing?

My mind was immediately flooded with images of women cross-legged on a platform overlooking my ideal pond, the water lapping against a dock, lilies floating, blue sky reflected in the still water, all basking in the warm glow of the sun disappearing behind the trees.

He coughed politely, bringing me back to the moment. The timing was perfect. Hans was away and he'd left me with an emergency stash of cash.

Soon, Sergio and I were walking the land together. We both agreed that the best location for a pond was on the west side of the property, where there was an unimpeded view of the setting sun.

Sergio was handsome and charming, as is often the way with Italian men, and so I jumped into bed with him. Kidding! But I did hand over a large cash deposit, money up front to secure lumber for the meditation platform and a dock (even though the pond would be far too small for boats), machine rentals and labour. All this without a word to my unsuspecting beloved.

By eight o'clock the next morning, a monster digger was scooping out the site, spitting out earth and boulders. Sergio had enlisted three additional men, all resembling male models in army fatigues, who had jumped straight into the work. When I came out to view the progress, Sergio waved and marched towards me, carrying a basket of fresh figs and a pot of honey, which he presented to me.

"*Principessa*, this is a gift from my farm," he announced, and then trotted back to join the *ragazzi*.

The following days were a joy: the company of gorgeous men, my pond gradually morphing into reality before my eyes, and daily treats from Sergio. By the end of the second day, they'd dug a mammoth hole the size of a tennis court and artfully placed the boulders they'd unearthed, some as big as Range Rovers, around the perimeter. By the third day, a gigantic black plastic liner carpeted the bottom and walls of the crater. And that's when Hans arrived home.

With great fanfare, I revealed the new project to my jet-lagged and grumpy husband. It did not go well.

"What have you done?" he asked, aghast.

"It will be the new meditation pond," I chirped.

"Where is the water?"

"Oh, don't worry," I said. "Sergio has everything figured out. You will love him. He brings me gifts of honey and fresh figs, and . . ."

"Who is Sergio?" Hans interrupted.

Since, as mentioned, the natural spring is on the other side of the hill, Sergio's brilliant plan was to truck in the water we needed. Over the following weeks, we filled the pond about forty times. Each delivery of water cost hundreds of euros, and each time it leaked slowly away. It was like trying to hold water in a kitchen colander. Cracks appeared in the liner, followed by thick, pointy weeds pushing their way through the plastic.

Within a month, Sergio, the specialist pond builder, had disappeared and Hans had stopped the water delivery before it bankrupted us. Since then, the pond has remained a stagnant, muddy mess, a happy home for mosquitos. Not even I had the enthusiasm left to try to fix it, though friends, family and guests made lots of suggestions. Why didn't we fill it in, build an amphi-theatre, a helicopter pad, a skateboard park, or buy pigs and let them enjoy the mud.

Then, one evening, Hans was in a romantic mood. Holding both my hands and looking deep into my eyes, he said, "Let's give it another go."

"Our marriage?"

I was a little confused.

"No, let's rebuild the pond. Let's try again."

So here we are this spring, like newlyweds, alongside Paolo, a human bulldozer of a man who has every young boy's dream job. Atop his digger, he builds roads and digs ditches, and also ponds for the local farmers. Why hadn't I ever talked to Paolo? He'd even worked on the property in the early days, doing everything from moving olive trees to smoothing out the gravel driveway.

Surveying the site, he shakes his bald head and shouts out one word: *"Argilla!"*

Clay, apparently, is the solution.

"What madman would use plastic?" Paolo laughs, slapping his thick thigh. A pond lining, he explains, should be natural clay, sensible and easy to do, since there is an abundance of the stuff around here—it's been used for centuries to make Tuscan terracotta pots.

Hans has fallen silent, likely absorbed in thoughts of murder, followed by the digging of clay graves for Sergio and me. I should have done my research.

We agree that Paolo and crew will rip out the plastic and line the walls and bottom of the hole with the local grey clay known as *argilla*. Now, when the level goes down in the hot summer months due to evaporation, we will see earth, not black plastic. Paolo also plans to dig a trench and lay pipe to enable us to pump spring water from the other side of the hill into the pond, which, as well as being a better way to top it up, will keep the water oxygenated. We will then be able to add fish, which will rid us of the mosquitos. Isn't nature wonderful?

Lesson learned: always opt for generations of local knowledge over smarmy good looks.

As the pond operation gets underway, I head to the market on a mission. Now that the first strawberries of the season are arriving in Tuscany from southern Italy, this afternoon I will treat my forgiving Hans and our saviour, the gentle giant Paolo, to my heavenly strawberry tiramisu. I smile at the vision of a bus full of plump, rosy strawberries shouting from their seats as the bus pulls in, "Here we are, here we are!"

The market takes place every Thursday in a field behind the Montepulciano bus station. You cannot miss it. The crowds arrive by foot, in overstuffed buses and cars, on bicycles and scooters.

Everyone is on a mission to acquire the freshest veggies, the plump-est fruit and their weekly fish; the morning's catch, just come in from the coast, will be sold out within an hour.

When I get there, the parking lot is already full, as is every street leading to the market. Watching these shoppers park is, as they say, like waiting for an accident to happen. Drivers scream profanities at any car or pedestrian blocking their progress. I am sorry to say that the women, especially the older ones, are the worst. They park in all directions and very often leave the motor running whilst they dash to the market.

As I attempt to find a spot where I won't get dinged, an old Fiat Panda, the most common car around here, backs into a sapling with enough force to snap it in half. The driver repositions her car, and off she trots, oblivious to the damage to both tree and vehicle.

I look around and find the supermodel of a policewoman who usually patrols the area, who also seems oblivious to what

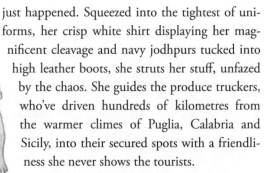

just happened. Squeezed into the tightest of uniforms, her crisp white shirt displaying her magnificent cleavage and navy jodhpurs tucked into high leather boots, she struts her stuff, unfazed by the chaos. She guides the produce truckers, who've driven hundreds of kilometres from the warmer climes of Puglia, Calabria and Sicily, into their secured spots with a friendliness she never shows the tourists.

I tingle with excitement as I weave my way through the crowds, past stalls of spades, machetes, trowels and seed trays, towards the strawberry vendor. Multicoloured linen dresses hang optimistically, waiting for summery days, and shoe stands have replaced their stock of winter boots with sandals and espadrilles.

A merry-go-round of memories hits me of my own days as a market trader—oh no, not working the money markets of Wall Street, but at a market stall with my best friend, Jacky. Since I met her while modelling in Tokyo, our lives have been entwined through thick and thin; she and her late husband, Steve, were crucial partners from the first moment I dreamed of offering retreats for women in my villa in Tuscany (before I even had a villa). After we were both back in London, we sometimes went weeks without a modelling assignment, so we supplemented our income with a variety of entrepreneurial ventures, all dismal failures.

One day, Jacky appeared at my door and pointed to her car, parked nearby. It was jammed with garbage bags, each one filled with T-shirts. She explained that her dad, who owned a garage, had been given them by a client in exchange for work done, and had asked her if she would like to take them off his hands.

"We could sell 'em," she said. "There must be about a thousand T-shirts in there."

The following weekend, as the sun rose over London, two excited young women headed to one of the city's hippest markets, Camden Town. We'd managed to scrape together the rent on a stall for the day, a trestle table well positioned amongst artisans selling everything from homemade jewellery to amateur paintings.

And that is how the drama unfolded that nearly had both of us tossed in the clink.

Jacky set off to find us breakfast while I prepared the table, setting out a cash box with a notepad and pencil beside it for jotting down our future sales, and practising my banter: *Roll on up, bargain of the century, sexy T-shirts for sale.* Soon Jacky returned with steaming coffees and two chip butties. (I highly recommend this British delicacy: fat, greasy french fries, sloshed in ketchup, between two slices of white bread. Absolutely zero nutritional value, but a perfect way to greet the dawn of our new career as market vendors and future millionaires.) After we demolished them, we opened the bags. The T-shirt on top was fine, but the next one and all the others underneath were unrecognizable as anything one could wear. They were shredded. Panicked, we tried the next bag, and the next, until we'd scrambled through the lot. You couldn't give this rubbish away. Jacky's dad had been ripped off, and so had we. Doomed and despondent, we started to pack up.

Then we heard a friendly cockney voice: "What are you gals doing here?"

We looked up to see Michael, a fashion photographer we'd both worked with. After we told him the dismal tale of two failed businesswomen, he said, "Don't get your knickers in a twist. I've something you can sell!"

Michael lived right around the corner from the market. Leaving Jacky to guard our stall and pack up the tattered T-shirts, I followed him to his flat, currently home to a mountain of cardboard boxes. He opened one up and took out a white camisole trimmed with broderie anglaise. It had hook-and-eye fasteners down the front and two small pockets. I flung off my shirt—I was perfectly comfortable stripping off in front of photographers—and put it on. It was beautiful.

"Take the lot and sell them," Michael said.

"But we have no money!"

Michael told me not to worry. "Pay me after you've sold them."

He helped me carry four large boxes to the market and headed back to his flat for more while we unpacked the lot. They were so pretty and came in most sizes. The only hitch was that they were dusty, especially inside the front pockets. They didn't smell or seem dirty in any other way, so no problem; I was sure they would sell. We just shook them out and piled them decoratively on the table, Jacky and I each slipping one on so we could model them for our customers, the first of whom were the nearby stallholders, who each bought one.

We also felt lucky because of the weather. England is renowned for grey drizzle, even in the summer, but this weekend was not only abnormally hot, there was not a cloud in the sky. As the sun shone down on our bare shoulders, we sold camisole after camisole to passing shoppers. At first, we asked for a fiver each, but by lunchtime we'd confidently doubled the price. By mid-afternoon there wasn't a camisole left. We counted the takings and then treated ourselves to hot dogs. Driving home, we sang our hearts out, imagining retiring by the time we were twenty-one.

I called Michael to tell him of our glorious success and offer him his share of the takings. He told me not to worry about that for now—he had plenty more camisoles for us to sell. So the following Saturday, there I was on his doorstep, picking up more boxes. This routine carried on for a month: pick up the camisoles, shake out the dust, pile them on the table and sell, sell, sell. The sun kept shining too, and we were doing so well, we soon splashed out on a full-length mirror and hung a curtain around the top of a metal stand for the punters to try on the tops. We wore bum bags (aka fanny packs, but the word "fanny" is considered very rude in England), so we could stash the takings more swiftly. There was no stopping us.

The fifth weekend arrived. By this time our success had us envisioning not only moving to the Caribbean but also the size of the yacht we'd buy once we got there. I got to Michael's to find police tape surrounding the building. Ducking under it, I dashed up the stairs to his front door and rang the bell. It opened a few inches and a woman peeked out. "Run," she whispered, and I did, right back to the market and Jacky. Quickly, we gathered our stuff and went home.

The following day, the front page of the British newspapers had photographs of Michael and some other dodgy blokes being handcuffed. Another picture showed Michael's bathtub piled full of what looked like a mountain of white sugar. Michael and his cronies had been importing cocaine from South America in the pockets of the camisoles we'd been selling. They received a seven-year jail sentence, and our retail venture skidded to a halt.

But I still have a real fondness for street markets.

I carry my bounty of strawberries towards the car, inhaling their intoxicating scent. The Sicilian vendor's fruit, which is trucked in from Sicily, is sublime, but he has a fondness for handing over the goods at the same time as grabbing your free hand to pull you towards him to plant a soggy kiss on your lips. Today I foiled him by holding my shopping bag out to his more virtuous son, who filled it to the brim with the reddest, juiciest strawberries.

Back home, I'm in the process of hulling the fruit for the tiramisu when I hear shouts coming from the direction of the pond. Rushing out to investigate, I find Hans and the *rigazzi* screaming instructions to one another as they attempt to remove sheets of the defunct pond lining. It's a filthy, toilsome task. Dragging ten-metre-long strips of algae-coated plastic up and out onto dry land unleashes the putrid smells of a harbour on a stinking hot day. Then they have to hook the muddy sheets onto Paolo's digger so he can haul the dripping plastic away, a process that whips them through the air, coating everyone and everything in slime.

Hans and the gang now resemble hideous swamp creatures from old movies. This is not the time to suggest that they all stop for a celebratory picnic of tiramisu and cups of Earl Grey. Waving encouragement, I retreat to the kitchen, wondering what I can do with all those strawberries.

Thankfully, they will not go to waste. As the work comes to an end for the day, Paolo tells me there is a *festa* that evening in his nearby village to welcome spring and celebrate their saint—there is almost always a saint involved in the local communal parties. He asks us to join him and his family, and to bring the promised tiramisu. I've bought so much fruit, I end up loading five large dishes of creamy strawberry deliciousness into our car.

Communal dinners are frequent across Italy, especially in rural areas. They are passionate, lively affairs where three to four generations of friends and neighbours come together over their love of each other and of food. Long trestle tables are set up along the entire length of the *corso*, or main street—usually narrow, cobbled and wide enough for horse and cart, not a car. Some *festas* seat over a thousand diners at one long table that snakes through the town. These parties celebrate saint's days, but also everything from chocolate, garlic, truffles, olive oil and wine to *la Festa dei Nonni*, the annual festival honouring grandparents.

Tonight's party in Montisi, Paolo's medieval village, will feed about a hundred hungry souls—and hungry is what you are required to be. Just drop twenty euros into the charity box and you are welcome. Getting all the food on the table is highly organized chaos. The *nonne* perform their gastronomic skills in the school kitchen—chopping, frying, roasting, boiling and berating anyone who dares get under their feet. The mums dance between guests, serving course after mouth-watering course. Fairy lights twinkle above red-and-white-checked tablecloths cluttered with glasses and unlabelled bottles of wine donated by local farmers. Because the evenings are still chilly, piles of throws are folded on benches for us to wrap up in.

The menu is always *la cucina povera*, peasant food, uncomplicated and homemade, food for the soul. Served first is a humble slice of toast. Don't be disappointed—it is divine, even though local bread is tasteless because the bakers don't add any salt. During the Roman age, salt had more value than gold and so was too costly to add to bread. (Roman soldiers were often paid with pouches of salt, not coin. In fact, the Italian for "salt" is *sale*—sounds like *sall-ay*—a word that is the origin of *salary*. How's that for great trivia!) Traditions hold fast here, so Tuscan bread is still saltless, but that makes it ideal as an edible utensil to scoop up thick ribollita soup or to hold piles of chopped tomatoes for bruschetta or the toppings of hundreds of varieties of crostini. Tonight's bread is toasted, rubbed with a clove of garlic, drizzled in olive oil proudly donated by one of the larger olive farms nearby, and then sprinkled with coarse salt. Devoured along with gulps of red wine, the dish is designed to wake up the senses for the impending feast.

Next, platters of antipasti arrive, piled with prosciutto and salami bequeathed by the town's butcher, and slices of pecorino, Tuscany's speciality sheep cheese. There is stagionata, aged, tangy, and strong, and then *fresca*, fresh young cheese, delicate and sweet. (My favourite of the cheeses is the rich, blue-veined Gorgonzola.) Then come crostini ("little crusts"), displayed on cake stands and greeted with gasps. Tonight's varieties feature crushed pea pesto with mint, liver pâté, grilled mozzarella mixed with chopped walnuts in honey, and marinated mushrooms with feta (another of my favourites). People eat, drink, chat with their neighbours and shout to each other from either end of the long table. The top button of my jeans pops open just as silence descends for the dramatic arrival of the *primo*: lip-smacking bowls of steaming pici pasta, a distinctly homemade, traditional Tuscan dish of thick, wormlike strands of pasta designed to hold a thick *cinghiale* ragù.

*Cinghiali*—wild boar—are my daily curse, sneaking up from their home in the chestnut woods in the early hours of morning to maraud the villa grounds, using their bristly snouts as shovels as they search for juicy grubs. Families of *cinghiali* have destroyed my flower gardens and lawns many times. (More about these beasts later.)

The whole crowd wolfs down the pasta with gusto, but for me, this is revenge eating.

As the church bells strike midnight, hours past our usual bedtime, the *secondo* makes its grand entrance: grilled vegetables drizzled in olive oil, crisp roast potatoes and the queen of the meal, gargantuan Fiorentina T-bone steaks, which are paraded around on wooden boards and then sliced and served. The butcher, Signore Belli, arrives and takes a bow. He has both supplied and grilled the magnum opus, meat from the famous white Chianina cattle raised in a nearby valley. If you are a meat eater, this steak is the very best.

By now I am going cross-eyed from exhaustion and over-indulgence. I would quite happily join the granddad opposite me, who is snoring, his head resting on a slice of eggplant squished into the table. Several children have also run out of steam and are passed out in their mothers' arms. Others are more energetic, including the pharmacist, a man of considerable girth, who is playing his accordion in the piazza. Some of the diners are working off their dinner by dancing to his tunes.

Then comes my tiramisu, announced by Paolo, now scrubbed clean, who tells everyone it has been made by the *straniera*, the foreigner. They all cheer, though I know locals find it hard to believe that an English woman's cooking might be edible. Delighted, I watch them gobble it up.

Grabbing Hans, I leave the hard-core revellers to glasses of *digestivo*, and we follow our stomachs home.

# STRAWBERRY TIRAMISU

SERVES 8

*Everyone has a different method for making tiramisu, but the absolute standout at our retreats is the one we make during strawberry season, in the cooking class taught by Chef Francesco. It's such an easy recipe, and the berries give it a zingy touch. Even better, you don't have to turn the oven on.*

**Simple Vodka Syrup:**
1 cup water
1 cup granulated sugar
½ teaspoon vanilla extract
2 ounces (60 ml) vodka

**Strawberries:**
4½ cups strawberries, hulled and sliced in half

**Mascarpone Custard:**
4 egg yolks
½ cup granulated sugar
2½ cups crème fraîche
2 cups mascarpone cheese
60 to 70 ladyfinger biscuits
Unsweetened cocoa powder (optional)

*To make the simple vodka syrup:* Add the water to a small pan over medium heat. Add the sugar and vanilla and stir until the sugar dissolves. Add the vodka and simmer for 5 minutes to allow the syrup to thicken. Remove from the heat and let cool to room temperature.

*To prepare the strawberries:* Place two-thirds of the strawberries in a bowl, refrigerating the rest to use later. Pour the cooled vodka syrup over the strawberries in the bowl and set aside.

*To make the mascarpone custard:* Fill a saucepan one-quarter full with water and bring to a gentle boil. Add the egg yolks to a heatproof bowl that will fit on top of the saucepan, without touching the boiling water. Whisk in the sugar. Place the bowl over the saucepan of boiling water and whisk the mixture until thick. Remove from the heat and let cool slightly, then fold in the crème fraîche and mascarpone.

*To assemble:* Layer the ladyfingers in a 9- by 13-inch (23 by 33 cm) baking dish (or a similar size). Spread the syrup-soaked strawberries evenly on top. Spread the mascarpone custard over the strawberries. Refrigerate for a few hours.

TO SERVE: Scatter the reserved strawberries over the tiramisu and sprinkle with cocoa (if using).

"I blame my mother for my poor sex life. All she told me was
'The man goes on top and the woman underneath.'
For three years my husband and I slept in bunk beds."

—JOAN RIVERS

# A Human Sandwich and
a Happy Ending

The pond is finished and now we wait for rain to help top up the water being pumped up from the spring. There are more benefits to having your own pond than the sheer beauty of it. Eventually we hope to divert the grey water from the villa and guest suites through its reed bed and recycle it back to the showers. I also hope, with a clay lining rather than plastic, there will be a smorgasbord of grubs around its perimeter to satisfy the wild boar—no more dining out on the manicured lawns. And what about ducks? I have never had ducks; well, I've never had a pond, either.

The massage hut will now have a view of serene water rather than the slimy old mudhole, which will add to the relaxing experience. Countless tears have been shed inside its walls. We offer every retreat guest an Ayurvedic massage from Lalla, the massage therapist, who trained in the technique in India, where Ayurveda originated. The massage combines slow, rhythmic movement with deep pressure, soothing tired muscles and releasing emotions. Anger, grief, frustration, resentment, sorrow—all the feelings that make up the jigsaw of our complex lives—can pour out as a result, sometimes in an overwhelming fashion.

I often see Lalla standing outside the massage hut with a guest cradled in her arms. I remember joining her once to sit with a woman called Cynthia, a single mother whose thirty-year-old son had died in a mining disaster, as she cried inconsolably. When she calmed, she told us the massage was the first time she had been touched and held since he'd died. Her friends had found it awkward to be around her, let alone sit with her in her grief, which is a pretty common reaction.

That evening, during the *aperitivo*, she told the group about her son. She was hugged by everyone. At dinner that night, a fellow guest kept an arm gently draped around her, while another stroked her hand. At the end of the retreat, Cynthia told us her healing had finally begun, thanks to the immense power of sharing and the wonders of human touch.

The guys who come here for the classic car rallies rarely take us up on the offer of a massage, confirming the stereotype that they are far happier playing with the cars, their emotions neatly stored away. Hans too. He's guaranteed to scuttle off at the first hint of a wail escaping from the closed hut door.

But I adore them, especially when I'm travelling. Years of filming on location often found me far from home and lonely. I'd prefer to book an in-room massage, rather than spend the money on room service. A good therapeutic rubdown always leaves me relaxed and able to sleep like the dead, but there are different styles of massage and inept therapists, too, who are a waste of time and money. Too soft, too hard, too weird, too dull. Sounds rather like unsatisfactory sex.

I once had a treatment from an enormous Mexican massage therapist working at a spa in Arizona. Pedro used his body weight to pummel every fibre, giving an extraordinary treatment that was in high demand at the spa. By the time it was my turn at the end of a gruelling day, he must have been exhausted. Halfway through the massage, he fell asleep standing up. Picture this—and I warn you, it is not pretty: I am face down, naked apart from a pair of undies. Pedro is standing at my head, relieving the tension in my neck. I am wondering why the pressure seems to be getting weaker when he topples over—not on the floor but right on top of me! Jarred awake by the fall, he finds me squashed between him and the table. Neither of us was hurt, but poor Pedro was hugely embarrassed.

Then there was my massage experience in Vietnam, which still makes me roar with laughter. I will never forget it, and neither will a fellow traveller named Brian. I'll get to the massage story, but first let me tell you about the trip.

Ten years ago, Jacky and I volunteered for a charity trek to raise money for colon cancer research. Both of my parents and Jacky's father had died way too young from this dreadful disease. Along with a group of twenty trekkers—a diverse mix of colorectal nurses, doctors, media types, businessfolk and one set of honeymooners, Julia and the aforementioned Brian, all of whom had been touched by colon cancer in some way—we were flown halfway around the world to Vietnam.

After the arduous thirteen-hour flight from London to Ho Chi Minh City, old Saigon, the organizers suggested an evening walk. Since we were about to embark on a gruelling hike across the Central Highlands, covering thirty kilometres a day, Jacky and I decided to let the others explore the city—we would book the hotel's five-dollar massage instead.

We were met by two tiny ladies at the spa. In separate cubicles, we stripped off, put on the required disposable underwear and climbed onto our respective tables. Our massage therapists rubbed and pummelled away at our jet-lagged bodies as they gossiped and joked with each other through the paper-thin privacy wall. Some of their words needed no translation, such as *wobble, wobble* and *jiggly, jiggly*. Obviously, our oversized Western bodies were cause for hilarity. They walked on our backs and played with our bottoms as if kneading dough. Even so, it was extremely relaxing, and I dozed off. Towards the end of the massage, I was awakened by Jacky loudly whispering, "Debbie, when she asks if you would like a 'happy ending,' you say no—it's not what you think."

Jacky was right, I had no clue what that meant, and was grateful for the warning.

The next day, we took a second plane north, up into the magnificent Central Highlands, Cao Nguyên Trung Phần. (Say that after three martinis!) Spilled out underneath us lay a series of green and

fertile plateaus, home to coffee and silkworm farmers, surrounded by vast mountains. We were to walk an ancient trail that began on the border with Cambodia and headed east through villages of thatch-roofed houses on stilts, dense bamboo forests and wide rivers we'd need to cross on dugouts.

We landed on a short runway. No tarmac, just red dirt. Here, we were met by local guides, along with eight majestic elephants, standing patiently waiting, trunks swaying, with large crates on their backs. Our group squealed with astonishment and relief—we would be riding across the country, not walking. On elephants!

Not so, we soon found out. The crates would carry the luggage and tents. So off we went on foot, a herd of pale-faced Westerners.

Ho Chi Minh City had been chaotic. Crossing the road was terrifying. Thousands of scooters hurtle towards you from every direction, many loaded up with whole families of three, four or even five people balancing on one bike, or huge piles of goods. The whole colourful city, sparkling with an electric energy, set my heart racing and sent my nervous system into overload.

But it was peaceful on the trail, as if we'd entered a time warp where little had changed for centuries. We came upon Indigenous farming families living a simple, rural life. With shy, smiling faces, they welcomed us, this strange group of boot-clad, backpack-carrying foreigners. We hiked through villages where women held out large leaves from wild rubber plants, offering us slices of watermelon and papaya. As their children ran barefoot and laughing alongside us, we in turn handed out coloured markers. The kids used them to scribble on each other's naked chests, giggling, and then grinned as they posed for photographs. The few elderly people we came across seemed suspicious, or perhaps full of sorrow—survivors of the Vietnam War. They never came to speak with us, just watched

us from outside their homes or stayed where they were, bent over in paddy fields beneath the traditional conical hats called *nón lá.*

Ten days later, we mud-splattered, sweat-stained hikers flew back to the city. The bus taking us from the airport to our hotel bumped along potholed streets, every hole we hit exaggerating the pain in our tired bodies. Exhausted but exhilarated, we had completed a hike of over two hundred kilometres without incident, apart from weeping blisters, aching muscles and bad hair, and we had raised half a million British pounds for colon cancer research. The trip was illuminating, often hilarious and life-changing, and was about to be more so for poor Brian.

No one could deny that the inside of the steaming bus smelled like rotting vegetables. Showers had been rare and brief on the trek, and we were all desperate to scrub off the grime. I made the mistake of rattling on about the unbelievable five-dollar hotel massage Jacky and I had snuck in on the night before the trek: bliss. After we arrived at the Rex Hotel (famous for housing correspondents during the Vietnam War), the whole busload of hikers dashed straight to reception to book themselves a massage.

"What were you thinking?" cried Jacky. "There'll be no room for us."

As it turned out, it wasn't a problem. The hotel brought in a team of massage therapists so they could accommodate us all.

Showered and wearing the crackly paper underwear, twenty of us were led into our "private" cubicles and simultaneously rubbed down. Just the ticket: relaxing and soothing and ridiculously cheap.

An hour later, feeling human again, Jacky and I meandered back to reception to pay our five-dollar fee, to find Brian, one of the honeymooners, kicking up a fuss at the far end of the counter.

He was shouting, so it wasn't hard for all nineteen of his fellow trekkers to overhear.

"But everyone else paid five dollars. Why are you charging me fifty?"

The Vietnamese receptionist smiled innocently and put her hands together in a slight bow. "But, sir, you had happy ending." And then, just to kick him where it really hurts, she added, "If you prefer, you pay with Air Miles."

Honeymoon over!

"I am a marvelous housekeeper.
Every time I leave a man, I keep his house."
— ZSA ZSA GABOR

# Vroom, Vroom!

It is one of those wet days in Tuscany that reminds me of my English childhood. Staring despondently out the window at the valley obscured by fog and sleeting rain, I have a sinking feeling that all work will have to be cancelled today.

We'd planned to kick off the major spring cleaning this morning. This is no mean feat. All the outside furniture, enough to fill a showroom, needs to be washed down with soapy water, checked to see if it needs repairs, set to dry in the sun and then positioned in the spot where it will remain until the end of October. In the kitchen I find my army of scrubbers, Maryana, Mimi, Gabriella, Joy and Luca—a Ukrainian, two Romanians, a Brazilian and one Italian—standing at attention next to buckets and piles of rubber gloves.

"Go home," I say.

Away they march, already making plans for their unexpected day off.

Instead of sitting around brooding on what isn't getting done, Hans and I decide to head to France for an overdue meeting with

Fabien, who owns the fleet of cars we use for our week-long classic car rallies.

One of the immense pleasures of living in Europe is the privilege of hopping in the car on a whim and driving to another country, where a new culture and new food beckon. Start almost anywhere, and in the time it takes to drive between New York and Washington or from Toronto to Montreal, you will find yourself in another country. Italy borders France, Switzerland, Slovenia, Austria and the two tiny principalities of Liechtenstein and Monaco, all of them reachable in less than a day. And so much to experience when you get there!

I always want to warn the tourists I meet, usually on a plane, who tell me they are "doing" Europe in a week, that it is not like a portion of Disney World to be rushed around. "*Piano, piano*," as the Italians say—take it slowly, slowly. Savour the diversity of each country, take your time.

Occasionally, we drive all the way from Tuscany to the United Kingdom, which I wouldn't recommend, what with the ever-increasing cost of gas, the price of food along the way, tolls, at least one night in a hotel, and the exorbitant price of the Euro-tunnel. Why do that when you can take advantage of flights on the numerous discount airlines we are blessed with here? But we are also parents, so several times over the last couple of years we've packed up our car with a load of my elder son's stuff, which he had stored in our Tuscan garage while he was away on different missions abroad. He and his wife are humanitarian aid workers who help to improve the welfare of those displaced by war or hit by a natural disaster. But they are back in England for the foreseeable future now, and so we load his collection of Kenyan spears, woks from Sri Lanka, Sudanese pottery, sacks of Masai shawls, and robes from a tribe he once stayed with in Papua New Guinea, among other things, into the trunk and a box on the roof. You can imagine what fun we've had at customs!

On last December's odyssey, I left the planning for the trip to my husband, including where we'd stop for the night. At the time I was relieved—one less job for me. But after what happened, I will never again let Hans book our accommodation. Since the car was packed up with my kid's priceless belongings, his assignment was to find a hotel in Turin, on the border with France, with parking within its grounds. After a day of gruelling driving through frenzied Italian traffic, the sun was setting as we neared the hotel *he* had chosen (just making sure you're clear on this point).

Ahead of us was a mystical turreted castle looking out over a sprawling valley, with the city of Turin twinkling below.

"It looks lovely, dear," I said, silently amazed. "And so incredibly cheap. Wow, well done."

We drove through elaborate iron gates; the car and its eclectic contents would be safe here. We parked, grabbed our overnight bag and climbed the vast stone steps to the main entrance. But instead of a grand wooden door worthy of a castle, we were greeted by a sliding glass job that discharged elevator music on opening. The receptionist had a magnificent head of crimson hair with a balayage of florescent green ends from which peeped the head of the snake tattoo that crawled up her neck. Not judging—whatever gives you joy.

What did disturb us was the reception space itself. Rather than oak panelling on the walls and Renaissance frescos adorning the high ceilings of the cavernous space, the lobby was veneered in white plastic and illuminated by throbbing pink strobe lights. Gulping, we checked in, trying not to seem old. Nadia, the red-and-green-haired receptionist, was super friendly, confiding that there were eighty rooms but we had the place to ourselves. We were the only guests.

The elevator, the hall corridor and (yes, you guessed it) our room were all lit by the same pink strobes, accompanied by piped-in supermarket music. The room, stripped of any glamour, was a white box with a bed and a forlorn-looking plastic chair in the corner. Just outside our door was a vending machine the size of a Sub-Zero fridge. It sold one item that came in a variety of textures, flavours and colours. How relieved we were to discover that we had our very own condom dispensary. And if we were to run out during the night, there was one on each floor. Phew!

Miserable, hungry and cold (there was no heating), we headed to the restaurant to the tune of "Tie a Yellow Ribbon Round the Ole Oak Tree." I was ready to tie that bloody ribbon around the neck of my travel agent, who was desperately trying to avoid all eye contact.

We waited an eternity to be seated in a dining hall that could easily accommodate two hundred people. The tables were all laid, which seemed like a good sign. A lady who had been busy washing the floor at the far end of the room finally wandered over, mop in hand, and said, "*Chiuso.*" Even if you don't speak Italian, you've probably figured out that means "closed."

Still, she offered to bring us something to eat. Thirty minutes later, she shuffled back with a basket of plastic-wrapped crackers, cubed orange cheese, two bags of peanuts and a bowl of wrinkled olives emitting a strange whiff. She'd added a bottle of red wine, which we took back to bed, leaving the rest.

In case you're wondering, the place turned out to be a venue for low-budget weddings. Or maybe an equally unappealing brothel.

—

Back to today's outing! The south of France is only a five-hour drive—definitely no need to stop at the "love hotel" near Turin. When we get to Provence, we will stay in a stylish bed-and-breakfast, booked by me, and the following day meet up with our friend Fabien, a man who could only be French. We have worked together on several rallies, and I have to say I have never met a more smartly dressed gentleman. (I just know he has a fabulous relationship with his mirror. I imagine each morning he greets it with *"Bonjour, chéri. Tu es magnifique aujourd'hui."*)

During our rallies, his wardrobe changes throughout the day, forever matching, always impeccable, just like his car collection. It is quite incredible to watch someone who spends his days work-ing around cars and never see a smudge on their perfectly pressed yellow pants and crisp salmon-pink shirt. If a disaster involving car oil, dust or dirt should happen, he reappears minutes later in yet another ensemble worthy of the runways of Paris.

As soon as we hit the Tuscan coast, we leave the soggy grey gloom behind. Endless blue stretches beyond us as sea meets sky. The day has become so spectacular, it feels like we're on holiday. We decide to stop for a bite of lunch in Liguria, the region that butts between Tuscany and Piedmont. Liguria features some of Italy's most challenging terrain, where rugged mountains dip their feet into the Mediterranean Sea. The road slices through cliffs on either side, striped with terraces of cultivated crops. How on earth do they farm here? Pastel-coloured houses smile up from villages hanging precariously over the sea, with turquoise, pink and yellow boats sprinkling their tiny harbours. We spot a medieval hamlet clinging to a cliff edge, and Hans takes the next exit.

A hamlet is a little bigger than a *borgo*, yet smaller than a village. The ones in Liguria feature ancient clusters of homes built into the hillside. There is always a church, a small castle and a couple of villas that would once have housed the noble families. The rest of the inhabitants live in small stone houses whose front doors open directly onto the narrow streets. You will usually find the three Bs—a butcher shop, a bakery and a bar—to feed the locals and the likes of us, travellers dropping in on their way to other places, new faces for the elderly inhabitants to gossip over.

We park outside the village and huff and puff our way up the steep cobbled road, too narrow for our car. "Built for donkey traffic," Hans remarks, seconds before said donkey, well-laden, passes us, its owner tipping his cap and offering us a toothless grin. (Maybe because he enjoys the sight of tourists having to hoof it up to the village.)

How lucky we are! The first building we come across is *la panetteria*. We stand for a moment in the sunshine, catching our breath and looking around. We've stumbled upon heaven, a view that spreads out over the Mediterranean Sea, such a majestic panorama it moves us beyond measure. Tummies grumbling, we enter the bakery. A long glass counter is laid out with every possible type of our favourite flatbread, focaccia—including rosemary, basil, salami, Gorgonzola and tomato. We hadn't realized that focaccia originated in Liguria. We um and argh, trying to decide which one will be our lunch.

Then something typically Italian happens. The baker emerges from the back of the shop. Thrusting out a floury hand to shake, he introduces himself and then tells us he will make us our very own focaccia. We follow him into the back, realizing once more that these are the moments we dream of, the reason why we have chosen to live in this foreign land.

An enormous *forno*, a brick oven, dominates the kitchen. Mounds of dough lie lethargically on a marble slab. Antonio, our new friend, slices a chunk off one of them and rolls and flattens it into a rectangle. He shows us how to dimple the dough with our thumbs, then he brushes the surface with extra virgin olive oil, the excess collecting in the thumbprints. Next, he presses cherry tomatoes into the dough and sprinkles it all lavishly with coarse sea salt and fresh rosemary. Into the oven it goes.

I ask Antonio what the difference is between pizza and focaccia, given that the ingredients seem so similar. Jokingly, he throws his arms in the air, claiming that he is a *maestro*, a bread-making artist, not a *pizzaiolo*. He goes on to tell us that there is more yeast in focaccia dough, which makes the bread lighter and fluffier than pizza. The dimples he makes with his thumb hold in the moisture, and the toppings are always simple. Focaccia, he explains, is a snack or side dish, whereas pizza is generally a meal.

We thank him and wait outside, soaking up the spring sunshine while our snack bakes, and mulling over this latest unexpected experience. Minutes later, we are tucking into focaccia made just for us.

Well fed, we drive on. The traffic is heavy now. The sprawling port of Genoa, the gateway to the Riviera, is the main reason for the massive trucks clogging up the highway, but before long they veer off to the port and we sail on towards the border town of Ventimiglia.

The steep hills surrounding us are a botanical wonder. The area is known as the Riviera dei Fiori, the riviera of flowers; we pass mile after mile of glass greenhouses growing carnations, all to be shipped around the world.

Hans glances at me and smiles kindly. He knows where my mind has drifted; this is my grandmother's old stomping ground. She regularly drove here from her house in nearby France, but she didn't come for flowers. She came for gold, in the form of jewellery.

To finance her thirty years living as a part-time expat in the south of France, Joyce sold antiques and old jewellery at the markets back home in England. Here on the Continent, she searched for treasures. She found the fancy Cote d'Azur far too expensive for antique hunting, so she travelled over the border into Italy to scavenge for deals.

When my father was in the final stages of colon and pancreatic cancer, which he would not survive, the pressure on my mum, pregnant with my brother at the time, must have been incalculable. My sisters and I weren't aware of all that was going on, but during the summer school holidays my parents decide to send me, the eldest, away. I flew alone from Manchester to Nice as an unaccompanied minor, watched over by the British Airways flight attendants. I rarely received that much attention at home, so I was in heaven. My grandmother met me when I got off the plane, a woman who was always a rare and wondrous sight for a girl growing up in the industrial north of England. Dear Joyce didn't disappoint: she was wearing a Pucci kaftan, a floppy hat and massive sunglasses, a cigarette dangling from luscious red lips. She was a terrible driver, as I've mentioned, but I had no fear. I was ecstatic to be hurtling along roads lined with palm trees, candy-coloured villas and the sea—oh, the sea.

I was far away from home, but I felt safe with her by my side. I was eleven and she was forty-eight at the time, but we always got on well, more like friends than grandmother and granddaughter, with secret nicknames for each other. Naughty and Nice, that was us. I was Nice and she was Naughty, to put it mildly.

We swam in the sea and ate moules marinières with frites at beachside restaurants. She drank café au lait out of a bowl, and I had freshly pressed *jus d'orange*, and together we watched the world go by. A boyfriend appeared now and then, but she was mostly single at the time. She'd already been married three times (maybe four—none of us could keep up).

We also spent hours of every sun-drenched summer day in the company of her flamboyant male friends, exotic birds in their pastel-patterned outfits and chirpy voices. Her canaries, she called them affectionately, preferring their company to any other. These gay men relished her company too, fluttering around her and making her laugh with their wicked gossip and their outlandish clothes. In my innocence, I took it all for granted, surreal as it seemed to a kid from Lancashire in the 1970s.

Her friends often assisted her in scouting out antiques and bric-a-brac that would be profitable to sell. During these excursions, she left me alone in her charming little house in Vieux Roquebrun, a village high above the sea. I would keep myself cheerfully occupied, exploring the cobbled streets and playing with the local kids. We would eat baguettes dipped into melted chocolate in the kitchen of Madame Dubois, a neighbour who kept a watchful eye on me. My mother back home would have had a meltdown if she knew Joyce was leaving me alone, but who was telling? Certainly not Granny or me.

One day I sat on the edge of the bath, watching Joyce apply lipstick and lashings of mascara. She was getting ready to drive to Ventimiglia. Out of the blue, I plucked up the courage to ask if I could go with her. She had planned on going alone this time, with no entourage in tow. I nearly fell into the bathtub when she said yes. I'd never been to Italy. I'd never been anywhere except this one trip to see her in France and the occasional family holiday in Wales.

In those days, there were strict border controls between European countries, but we had no problem at customs. Fifteen minutes later, we arrived in Ventimiglia's grand piazza. She dropped me off, handed me a few lire for a sandwich and gelato, and told me she would be back soon. I was on my own. Of course, I had no cellphone back then, in case of emergency—it was just me and the buzz of life going on around me. So I did what preteens usually get up to: I hung out and made new friends.

Four hours later, Joyce returned, and we set off on the short journey back to France. On the Italian side of the border, we were pulled over by the *guardia alla frontiera*. I remember it like it was yesterday, and especially clear is what Joyce was wearing: a flouncy fuchsia silk blouse with long, flowing sleeves, tight white pants and gold flats.

The border guard told us both to get out of the car. Pointing to the trunk, he said, "*Aprilo*." Joyce did as she was told and opened it. Stepping back, she offered him her warmest smile. The guard did not smile back. He rummaged around inside for a minute; it was empty apart from our folded beach chairs. And then, with the trunk still open, he indicated the road ahead. "*Avanti*," he said, never taking his eyes off my grandmother.

Joyce reached up to close the trunk. The silky sleeve of her blouse slid down her arm, revealing ten gold watches.

Both of us were marched inside the customs station, where Granny was locked up until some powerful friends, including the mayor, with whom she had been especially friendly, pulled strings and had her released. I spent those hours happily playing backgammon with the border guards.

About ten years later, I told my mother the story, thinking enough time had passed that she'd find the whole scenario funny. She did not.

# LIGURIAN TOMATO AND OLIVE FOCACCIA

MAKES I FLATBREAD

*The ultimate focaccia should be light and pillowy, according to our new friend in Liguria. He explained that pizza is about what goes on top, whereas focaccia is all about the dough. To achieve the best focaccia, the dough needs to be wet, more like a batter. This dough is sticky and slightly runny, which makes it impossible to roll out, so instead you pour it into a baking pan.*

3¾ cups 00 flour (unbleached all-purpose will also work)
1¾ cups semolina flour
1½ tablespoons fresh yeast (or 2 sachets of dry yeast)
1 teaspoon fine salt
2 tablespoons extra virgin olive oil, plus more
    for oiling and drizzling
1 teaspoon brown sugar or honey
2½ cups tepid water
A handful of cherry or grape tomatoes, halved
A handful of pitted green olives, halved
Fresh rosemary leaves
1 teaspoon coarse salt

In a large bowl, mix together the 00 flour, semolina flour, yeast and fine salt. Make a well in the centre and add the olive oil. Stir the brown sugar or honey into the tepid water, then add it gradually to the flour mixture, stirring. The dough should be really sticky.

*continued...*

Add a little flour to your work surface and place the dough on it. Knead the dough until it becomes a little less sticky.

Oil a fresh bowl and place the dough in it. Cover it with a tea towel and let sit for about 1 hour. The dough should double in size.

Oil a shallow 9- by 13-inch (23 by 33 cm) baking dish. Tip the dough into the dish, stretching it to all corners. Cover with the tea towel and let sit at room temperature for another 30 minutes.

Preheat the oven to 425°F (220°C).

Now for the fun part! Using the end of your thumb, press fat dimples all over the dough. Place a tomato in half of the dimples and an olive in the other half, in whatever arrangement you like. Drizzle more olive oil over the focaccia, then sprinkle with rosemary and the coarse salt.

Bake for about 20 minutes, until golden. Remove from the oven and, while still hot, drizzle the entire surface with a little more olive oil.

TO SERVE: Cut into squares or place the whole focaccia on a board and let guests tear off chunks.

"Always get married in the morning. That way if it doesn't work out, you haven't wasted the whole day."

—MICKEY ROONEY

# A Happy Life Begins

So here Hans and I are, in France. Today there are no border controls, not that Hans and I are smuggling any illicit goods. As if! Within a blink of an eye, we hopped over the invisible line separating Italy and France. A few metres down the road, a sign announces *Bienvenue en France*, just in case a driver is in any doubt.

Before our meeting with Fabien tomorrow morning, we have an important dinner date. Dumping the overnight bag at the hotel, we change and head farther down the coast to Cannes. Michelin-starred restaurants are thick on the ground here, but they are not for us. We are heading to a particular hole in the wall. Its food is certainly not gourmet, and the service is mediocre, but we keep coming back to eat at La Porte Bleue. The first time we came here, the door really was painted blue. Tonight, we are greeted by a slug-brown one. But the colour of the door is irrelevant to us because this is the restaurant where we had our first date.

In a couple of weeks, the annual Cannes Film Festival will transform the town, turning it into a glamorous spectacle of chaos, dreams, greed and ambition. Another piece of travel advice: if you're not in the film business, avoid Cannes at all costs in mid-May. Every square inch is a mosh pit of buyers, paparazzi, writers, directors and producers, all tussling for attention. Movie legends, recent celebrities and aspiring hopefuls walk the long red carpet, waving to fans from around the world who flock to Cannes for a glimpse of their idols.

As Hollywood descends, hotels are at capacity and there's not a restaurant booking to be had. If you do happen to find a vacant table, take a peek at the menu. The original prices will be crossed out and replaced with new ones, four times as high, just for the festival. Oh, the delicious arrogance of the French. How can a bowl of spaghetti alle vongole (pasta and clams) possibly be worth two hundred euros?

You think I'm joking? I'm not. I guess if you are about to sign a multi-billion-dollar movie deal, you don't care about the cost of lunch!

Tonight we're lucky, though, and the streets are nearly empty. Hans and I walk arm in arm along the splendid and quiet Promenade de la Croisette, following in the footsteps of film stars who've been coming to the festival since it began in 1946. The legendary hotels—Le Carlton, Le Martinez and Le Majestic—glitter self-importantly in the evening sun, busy preparing for twelve days of sensational glitz, fantasy and scandal.

Compared to the legendary tales of the Cannes Film Festival, our story is inconsequential. But for us, it was the beginning of a new life. This is where we met, where our lives changed in an instant. I was working in film production in London, and Hans was a movie buyer in Montreal who bought the rights to distribute foreign films across the country. I was in my late twenties; he, in his mid-thirties. I will never in a thousand years understand how I had the gumption to get myself to Cannes, but I somehow managed to bully the production company I worked for to allow me to join the team attending the festival—a handful of us, all young and naive and determined to seize every opportunity. Not the business ones, no; we intended to absorb everything from this magnificent experience, from the screenings to the fabled parties.

The minute my feet hit the ground, I made it my job to hunt out invitations. The film companies held parties to celebrate their upcoming movies. Each event had a strict guest list, often chained to the wrist of a studio secretary, but through sheer bravado and ruthless ambition, I somehow managed to bag a handful of invites.

The first party on the first evening was boring, just businessmen sitting around doing, well, business. But while my small gang and I were there, we met a movie salesman who invited us to the launch party for the whole festival, where there would be free drinks, dancing and men. Twenty minutes later, I found myself face to face with my future.

My workmates and I were busy guzzling the complimentary bubby when I spotted a handsome man alone among the revellers. I grabbed two drinks from the tray of a passing waiter, sauntered over and offered him a glass. It was not love at first sight; it took three days.

I invited Hans to join our group for the rest of the evening, which he did, and when we parted, I promised to take advantage of a spare ticket he had for the much-in-demand Warner Bros. event to be held the next night.

The following day, I wandered around the film market, which is very similar to a normal market, but instead of fruit, vegetables

and cocaine-dusted camisoles, they sell movies. Completely disinterested in work, I scanned the halls, hoping to bump into this new guy, Hans, to make sure we were still on. I had just the outfit to wear to the party: a silky Nicole Farhi dress that had cost me two months' salary—knee-length, with a pattern of pink pastel flowers, innocent yet seductive—matching heels and a clutch.

The Croisette runs right along the sea front, but parallel to it is a popular shopping street with the most delectable and expensive French fashions. Only in France have I ever seen so many underwear shops all displaying a delightful mélange of suggestive silk undies, as delicious as the patisseries next door. With the remains of my meagre savings, I bought the prettiest bra and satin knickers I could afford.

Then I did a stupid thing. Grabbing a coffee, I met another guy. Later on, I found out he was a carpenter working on the construction of the temporary stands at the festival, but he gave me the impression he was a movie mogul and asked me if I'd join him at the Warner Bros. party. I will never know why I said yes—probably as a pathetic backup plan in case Hans didn't show up. The carpenter and I arranged to meet at ten that evening outside the Palais des Festivals.

Hours later, in my glam undies and new dress, I was on Hans's arm—a suave, cool, enchanting man with a smile and the wit to melt this simple London girl's heart. We began the evening at the aforementioned bistro, La Porte Bleue, since Hans could not afford the fancy places. I didn't care and neither did he. As we were about to leave, an elderly woman in Romani garb, a common sight in the wealthy towns of the Côte d'Azur, came over to us from a corner table. She took our hands in hers and said, "*Vous serez ensemble pour toujours*." Roughly meaning "You two will be together forever."

We laughed uncomfortably—seriously, we had only known each other for twenty-four hours.

We arrived at the grand soiree, which was being held on the grounds of an apricot-coloured villa next to the sea. It was the most wondrous place I had ever been. Over by a palm tree were William Hurt, Cher and Clint Eastwood, all chatting. Breathless, we made our way through a magical garden strung with fairy lights, past waiters carrying large trays of champagne to offer to all the beautiful people.

In the corner of the garden was a marquee housing a bar. I drank my first Bellini as Hans introduced me to people he knew. My attraction to him only grew; he seemed kind and truly interested in others, so sexy in a man.

Then the bubble burst. I felt a tap on my shoulder and turned around, and there was the guy from the coffee shop. He was smiling, evidently unruffled by my standing him up. He asked me to dance. Happy to be seen as in demand, I said yes. I told Hans, who smiled and turned back to his conversation. I walked ahead to the dance floor, a temporary structure at the far end of the garden. As we circled a large fish pond, Wham!'s "Young Guns (Go for It)" was belting out of the speakers, a dance song that was not only my favourite, but was produced by Jacky's husband, Steve Brown (I did say Jacky's life and mine were entwined).

All of a sudden, I felt a firm finger thrust under my shoulder blade. Whispering profanities, the carpenter roughly picked me up and threw me into the middle of the pond. His journey of revenge accomplished, he fled. I sat up in the slimy water. Thankfully, it was not deep, but my dress was ruined and my shoes were gone. Unhurt but mortified, I was rescued by the head of NBC television. A fatherly figure, he waded in and shepherded me to my unsuspecting real date at the bar.

It was the best night of my life.

Hans led me back to his hotel room as I sobbed attractively into his shoulder. My brand-new knickers, now soaking wet, just had to be removed . . .

Okay, the rest you can imagine.

The following day, with a definite spring in his step, Hans rented a car and told me we were driving to Italy for lunch. *So glamorous*, I thought.

We never made it. In one of the tunnels that cuts through the mountains of southern France into Italy, we got stuck in an eight-kilometre-long traffic jam. Over the next four hours, the vehicles and the tempers around us overheated. But not us—we fell in love in that tunnel.

We talked endlessly, planning our future. We'd have ten children (we had two), he would move to London (I moved to Montreal), we'd marry at my childhood home in Lancashire, which we did only a few weeks later, and we would live happily ever after, which we have.

I had spent the first twenty-eight years of my life unsure and uncertain. With Hans, everything felt just right.

We set off for Fabien's garage the next morning full of anticipation: this is the first time we've ventured to his treasure trove.

Down a narrow shopping street somewhere in the centre of Nice, we find the address, a rusty industrial door flanked by a butcher's shop and a small haberdashery. Surely this cannot be a garage storing priceless classic cars? Ooh la la!

The door opens on a cavernous space fitted with floor-to-ceiling shelves, not for jars of candies or folded designer sweaters, but for sparkling jewel-coloured cars. Nirvana for a car lover like Hans. Vintage Porsches, Ferraris, an Austin-Healey, a Bugatti, multiple Jaguars, a Mustang and even a vintage Rolls-Royce—a massive shelving unit of cars. We have already met some of these beauties at rallies we've held at our place, but we've never experienced the entire collection. Proudly, Fabien shows us around.

After the tour, we spend the next few hours planning the upcoming rally, including the routes the guests from Canada, Australia and the United States will drive. I'm not a car lover, particularly, but I know that experiencing the diverse Tuscan landscape from behind the steering wheel of a classic car is an extra-thrilling adventure.

As we are saying goodbye—making sure we shake hands with the whole team—a spanner falls from a shelf several feet above us and clips the back of Hans's head. He is fine, his head dribbling just the tiniest amount of blood, but just to be safe, one of the mechanics dashes to the grocery store and returns with a bag of frozen *petits pois* so we can ice the bump.

Back on the road to Tuscany, I press the peas against the swelling, which is now the size of a walnut. Hans has insisted he is fine to drive. He would much rather tackle the Italian roads with a bag of frozen peas on his head than be tortured by me behind the wheel. In the warmth of the sun beating through the car window, I soon become drowsy, sinking into my thoughts, smiling to myself over a secret about frozen peas.

I am known as an erratic driver, but my parking escapades once landed me in court. In the 1980s, I drove a second-hand Citroën Deux Chevaux, or 2CV, the frog-shaped car that became a symbol of the French "art of living." It is a mystery how this comical vehicle, offering rudimentary comfort and an engine hard-pressed to power a sewing machine, conquered the hearts of so many and became the must-have car throughout Europe. Mine was bright turquoise—the love of my life at the time, and a lot more trouble than any boyfriend.

It had been dirt cheap to buy, a wreck that had lived most of its previous thirty years on a farm in Belgium. The steering wheel was on the wrong side, the excuse I used for my many mishaps, and one of the back doors was sealed shut. There was straw stuck between the seats that I could never get out and a general *odeur d'animal*. The side windows were flaps that, if you needed fresh air, you had to push upwards and secure. It was a convertible, but there were no fancy switches to lower the roof. You had to get out of the car, roll the canvas back into a large sausage and pin it to the back of the trunk. All fine and dandy in sunny climes, but in the unreliable English summers, a downpour would have you paddling inside the vehicle before you had time to stop and raise the roof. Still, I adored this car and would sail around the streets of London, exploring neighbourhoods from Paddington to Putney, Primrose Hill to Peckham, posh to poor.

It was while driving my 2CV that I became fascinated by the diverse architecture and ethnic vibes of the city. I also had time on my hands between modelling jobs, which could be scarce. In my case, anyway. One afternoon, I was meandering around the Baker Street area, Sherlock Holmes's hood, and turned down a back road. When I stopped at a traffic light, I heard a rap on the window and turned to find a fellow model grinning at me, another gal not working. We decided to go for a coffee, so I pulled over. Though there was a long gap in the pavement between other parked cars, with large letters painted on it saying *No Parking*, I drove in nose-first and sauntered off with my friend, completely oblivious to the fact that my car was sitting in front of three massive, bright-red double doors, under a sign glaring *Fire Station*. (It is these stories of my stupidity and self-centred youth that stop me in my tracks any time I'm tempted to moan about "kids today." I was just as bad as any of them, if not worse.)

An hour later, I arrived back to find six burly firemen hoisting the little Deux Chevaux on their shoulders like pallbearers carrying a coffin. The red doors were wide open, with three fire engines loaded up and ready to go, sirens blaring. There was also a police car with flashing lights and an unamused London bobby, his ticket book and pen at the ready. My fine was astronomical—so expensive, in fact, that I had to ignore it.

Before I could whine "Illegal parking? How was I supposed to know?" I found myself in front of a magistrate. There I was, this idiot girl, nervously sitting on a bench alongside swindlers, thieves and prostitutes—basically, London's petty crime scene. Waiting next to me was Edith, an eighty-year-old wrapped in an oversized coat, even though it was midsummer. Huge blue eyes looked out from her angelic face, deeply crumpled from life's laughter, grief and love, scanning the proceedings. Then they settled on me.

"Don't worry, kiddo, you'll be fine," she said.

I began to cry.

"I'm going down this time," she said, still surprisingly cheerful.

"What did you do?" I asked.

"Caught nicking again," she replied. "I'm looking forward to some company in the slammer. It's lonely in my flat now that everyone I have ever loved has gone."

Then Edith told me the story of how she'd been arrested. Dressed in the same thick coat and woolly hat she was wearing now, she'd passed out on a supermarket floor. Shoppers gathered around her, and a doctor was located who'd been shopping at the time of the incident. He checked her vitals and declared, "This is strange. She is suffering from hypothermia." Strange it was, since it was summer, London was in the middle of a heat wave, and she was dressed for winter.

Puzzled, he removed her hat, under which, to everyone's surprise, were a frozen chicken and a bag of frozen peas.

When Edith came around, the doctor sat her up slowly. The store manager gave her a cup of tea and then called the police.

Edith was sentenced to six months in the clink. I got off with a slap on the wrist, though I had to pay that fine.

# TUSCAN PEA SOUP

SERVES 4

*A recipe in honour of Edith, and also because I love peas so much, I can't live without them! I eat fresh shelled peas sprinkled with salt, and I add them to most stews and soups. A pile of peas topped with a knob of butter, alongside a baked potato or a piece of grilled salmon, is my idea of heaven.*

*May in Tuscany gifts us plenty of fresh peas. The market stalls are piled with pea pods, and I can't think of anything better than spending a sunny half hour shelling peas into a bowl while listening to a podcast. Of course, if fresh peas are not available, frozen are good too. Just don't nick 'em, like Edith did!*

*Many recipes for pea soup add potato or grains, but I think both take away from the rich flavour of the spring peas themselves.*

*This velvety pea soup, which we serve at the villa, is easy to make vegetarian by substituting pine nuts for the pancetta. Served with crusty bread and butter, it makes a perfect lunch or an elegant starter at a dinner party.*

4 cups fresh or frozen peas
4 green onions, finely chopped
½ teaspoon salt
½ teaspoon freshly squeezed lime juice
1 tablespoon extra virgin olive oil
½ cup finely diced pancetta (or 2 tablespoons pine nuts)
4 tablespoons plain yogurt
A handful of chopped fresh mint
Freshly ground black pepper

To a large pot of boiling water, add the peas and green onions. Reduce the heat and simmer for 10 minutes. Drain, reserving a cup or two of the cooking water, and return the vegetables to the pot. Add the salt and lime juice, then use a hand blender to purée the mixture. The soup should have the consistency of thick cream. If it seems too thick, closer to a pesto, blend in some of the reserved cooking water until it's the consistency you prefer.

In a small frying pan over medium-high heat, heat the olive oil. Add the pancetta and fry for a few minutes, until brown and crispy on the edges. Transfer to a plate lined with a paper towel. (Or, for the vegetarian version, toast the pine nuts in a small frying pan over low heat until just browned. Be warned: they burn easily! Transfer to a plate to cool.)

TO SERVE: Ladle the soup into bowls and top each portion with 1 tablespoon of yogurt. Add a spoonful of either pancetta or pine nuts to the middle of each bowl. Sprinkle with mint and pepper to taste.

"Dogs have boundless enthusiasm but no sense of shame.
I should have a dog as a life coach."

— M O B Y

# "A" Is for Alfie

My thoughts are whirling. I lean against the wall of the barn, watching the evening sky turn from blue to violet. What should we do? Can we do it again? Will we fall in love only to fail once more?

We'd just returned from the quick jaunt to France when my phone rang. I picked up, immediately recognizing the gentle Italian voice on the other end.

"I have a puppy for you," Fabrizio said. "He is perfect."

Fabrizio has the calmest of temperaments, which serves him well in his two contrasting jobs as an air traffic controller at Rome airport and a breeder of champion border collies. "The father of this puppy is the same dog as Alfie's."

The pain that shattered our hearts seven months ago is still with us. Neither Hans nor I are the type to go overly gaga about other people's pets, but the traumatic experience of losing our first-ever dog, a beautiful border collie we named Alfie, has left us with a true understanding of the genuine love people feel for their pets and the joy and comfort animals bring to our lives. When I shared the story of the accident that cost Alfie his life, I received messages of condolence from thousands of people, who laid bare their own grief in an effort to soothe ours. They all knew that slow, hollow pit in your stomach when you lose a dog, and the weight of the knowledge that he will never come bouncing into the room again.

Seven months ago, Hans was in a café on the side of the road with a friend, Alfie resting on the ground beside him. A cat ran out in front of them, and Alfie dashed after it, pulling the leash out of Hans's grip. A van hit him. A split second stole our friend from us.

But we count our blessings. Alfie's innocence and the joy he found in each moment of every day touched us, leaving us grateful for the short time we had with him. His grave lies in a corner of the cutting garden, surrounded by flowers.


My dog-owning adventures began because of Instagram. People say social media can be a dive into a deep, dark hole, and this is true. But it can also open up a world of new interests. A few years ago, I became fascinated by a particular border collie who has his own account. I know, what a world we live in!

Anyway, his name is Roman. He lives in Scotland, and his owner posts pictures of the two of them walking the majestic Highlands. I envisioned myself doing the same, only over the hills of Tuscany. I messaged Roman, and he wrote back—clever dogs, these borders. He explained that his kind originated in a rural area straddling Scotland and England called the Borders. Popular as a hiker's paradise thanks to rugged hills of captivating natural beauty, the Borders are also home to thousands of sheep. And with sheep comes the working border collie, the most intelligent dog breed of them all. Their overwhelming herding instinct and quick learning skills make them sought-after on sheep farms from Australia to Canada.

Roman soon introduced me to a breeder of border collies in Italy—Fabrizio. His speciality is show dogs, prettier and not quite as energetic as their working cousins, but with the herding instinct still intact. In Alfie's case, his instincts were usually triggered by children and innocent old ladies out for a stroll. Fabrizio's dogs make for loving and almost painfully loyal pets, but they still require oodles of exercise, both mental and physical.

Before he would grant us the care of a puppy, Fabrizio visited the villa to see if we would be suitable as parents. We passed, although I believe it was because of the amount of land we own rather than our nurturing personalities. A few months later he called to say he had a handsome puppy with a sweet nature that he thought would be just right for us.

This was the summer of 2021. It was not the ideal time to take on the challenging task of puppy training for the first time: we were in a state of pandemonium. My two sons, whom I love dearly, had recently declared that they were each getting married; happiness reigned. Then they each made their dream wedding request: they wanted us to host their respective celebrations at our home, something to warm a parent's heart. Then came the kicker: the weddings were scheduled within two months of each other during a global pandemic.

We smothered our shock with fake delighted faces. Then I courageously suggested a joint wedding. This went down as though I had offered to move in with them. They also nixed the idea of delaying one of the weddings for a year because of the pandemic. No way. So, along with our new puppy, we took on the typical trials and tribulations of planning and hosting both weddings, with the added considerable wrinkle of adapting to the forever-changing Covid rules.

Both events were stupendous, and as the old saying goes, that year we didn't lose sons but gained precious daughters. And one black-and-white border collie.

Everyone who has ever owned a dog knows they will steal your heart. Alfie was a head-turner. Intelligent, playful and comical, he had the darkest of chestnut eyes, which seemed to look straight into the soul. As a first-time dog parent, I was on the phone constantly with Fabrizio for advice. As I mentioned, he is an air traffic controller. The conversations went something like this:

"Ciao, Fabrizio, sorry to bother you. I have a question."

"That is okay, Debbie, but I am at work."

"Oh, it won't take a minute. Alfie has just eaten wild boar poo. What should I do?"

"Please hang on one second."

Then I'd hear his voice announcing to a pilot in the skies above Rome, "Delta 429—approaching runway four—please proceed to landing." Followed by a silence and then, "Okay I am back. Right, take some salt . . ."

This went on for several months. I am fully aware that if there had been a catastrophe at the Rome airport during this stretch, I would have been responsible.

Over the following fourteen months, we took Alfie everywhere with us. We even explored areas of Italy that we'd put off time and again but now wanted to see reflected through his eyes.

—

We were obsessed with our dog and became the ultimate bores. I told anyone who would listen, "It took me years to potty-train the boys, but Alfie only needed three days." And "Honestly, he is brighter than a toddler—he knows the name of every toy. Seriously, I think he'll be reading soon."

Alfie was a social pup, befriending all the retreat guests and even becoming a comfort dog to those in despair. We have our share of broken birds who stay with us in their quest to reboot their lives. I remember Amanda, young and recently widowed, struggling to pick up the pieces. At the beginning of the retreat, she often sat alone. Alfie would meander over and gently lay his head on her lap, closing his eyes as if absorbing her sorrow. When she was leaving at the end of the week, she told me she felt ready to rebuild her life, thanks to Alfie. She said, "His comfort has given me purpose."

And then, just before he turned sixteen months old, Alfie was hit by that truck on a country road. He was killed immediately, and there was not a scratch on his silky body, so he didn't suffer. Life went back to the way it was, just the two of us.

Now Fabrizio is telling me he has another border collie puppy who is just right for us. I attempt to push away the wave of sorrow. We have decided not to have another dog, convinced we do not have the courage to start again. We failed Alfie, and our confidence is nil. Still, I find myself agreeing to visit the new puppy in June. No promises, though.

> "You are never too old to set another goal
> or to dream a new dream."
> —C.S. LEWIS

# What Do Women Want?

The month of May is named after Maia, the goddess of spring. In my childhood village, on the first day of May a painted pole was erected in a field. Long coloured ribbons were strung from the top, and all the children danced merrily around, as they had done for centuries. May Day was a time to celebrate togetherness and the return of spring.

May at the villa means flinging open the doors to a feast of adventures in the belief that we'll all still be smiling and speaking to each other by the end of the hospitality season. We are about to kick off the first Tuscan Girls' Getaway of the year, and this beehive is abuzz.

Twenty excited guests are presently en route from Rome. Fortunately, the team has remained the same since we began running the retreats in 2015. Chef Francesco has once again taken up his role as commander of the kitchen. There are also five helpers, one yoga instructor, two massage therapists, a meditation teacher and my best friend, Jacky, wearing two hats: host and nutritional therapist.

Villa Reniella is impeccable inside and out, not a leaf out of place. I'm especially proud of the newly renovated terrace, where we'll soon host the first of many *aperitivi.* The restored *piccolo lago*, glistening below the villa, is as I had imagined, brimming with fish and floating lilies and even the occasional wild duck dropping in for a splash.

I have to admit, after all these years, it still feels peculiar when strangers take over the property after the freedom of us rattling around alone during the cooler months. But the thrill of hosting the retreats outweighs any misgivings.

At this precise moment, these women are taking in the verdant scenery through the van windows. Tuscany is blessed with a unique landscape, the drama of which has been depicted in many movies. Writers and poets—Chaucer, Dante, D.H. Lawrence, C.S. Forester, Henry James and Byron, to name just a few—have all been inspired by the inexhaustible beauty. I imagine the guests entranced by roads lined with majestic cypress trees, fields painted in poppies, purple cyclamen, cornflowers and daisies, a pilgrimage of colour. They'll see the craggy mountains, the spine of Italy, rising in the far distance, their peaks holding on to the last covering of snow. But it is the iconic rolling hills of Tuscany, cradling vineyards and olive groves, that will capture their souls.

The group will be tired after their long journey to get here, but as the vans turn down our kilometre-long driveway, I know they will gasp at the first sight of the villa waiting amongst the olive trees. Each passenger has envisioned the moment when she'll arrive at this tiny kingdom steeped in history, and Villa Reniella won't let them down. Nearly a thousand years ago, it was built as a lookout tower, a base for one solitary soldier. For centuries after, it was the home of families farming the land. Now it embraces women from all walks of life and is the catalyst for their shared stories, their hopes and their dreams.

As the vans come into sight, the Tuscan tribe is here to greet them. We wave, trays of chilled Prosecco at the ready, as the women tumble out into the sunshine. My heart swells. I know how important this week is for all of them.

The tempo shifts as if the villa has been plugged in. The music is on, drinks are inhaled and squeals of laughter ring out amid the hugs and introductions. We have perfected a routine for the arrival. While the guests and the team get to know each other, I lead each woman to her room. This gives me a chance to have a private moment with them, but it also boosts my ego to see them react to the spaces I have designed for the sole purpose of bringing joy.

When I jumped into this venture over a decade ago, I asked myself, "What do women want?" The answer was clear: a place to feel special, safe and inspired. Spurring my creativity with the worry that I'd fall short, I vowed to make the experience of staying at the villa perfect.

Before a retreat week kicks off, I spend a morning pretending to be each guest. I enter her suite through the private garden, envisioning how she will feel in this foreign place. I sit on the bed, imagining her curled up amongst the Italian linens, gazing through open shutters across the valley towards the medieval town of Montepulciano or up to the castle in the village behind us, illuminated against an evening sky.

It doesn't always go as planned. One year, I was standing in the entrance of one of the suites, chatting to Cynthia from Pennsylvania as she eagerly explored the room. She suddenly blurted, "Do you have snakes in Italy? I loathe snakes!"

I explained that, yes, there are snakes, but a sighting is rare. At that exact moment, my eye caught a movement above me. A metre-long green-and-yellow-spotted serpent had wrapped itself around the inside of the door frame. With visions of Cynthia legging it back to the United States in hysterics, I grabbed the hanging tail and flung the bewildered thing into the bushes. Somehow, Cynthia did not notice.

"Right, then," I said. "See you back on the terrace when you are unpacked."

The task of spending time inspecting each room is a lesson I learned from a hotel owner in Jamaica whose five-star Half Moon resort—fancy suites and villas—was spread across sprawling grounds. It was run by an Austrian couple, Klaus and Natasha, both absolute perfectionists. We filmed an episode of *The Painted House* there, and I became friendly with Natasha, who'd designed the interiors herself. In her late thirties, always stunningly put together, she had a fiery passion for the Caribbean paradise. The suites were "plantation style": mahogany four-poster beds, crisp white linens and framed botanical prints of the local flora on the walls.

Over a drink one evening, she explained to me that she spent a month each year making a round of the immense property to check out every room. One day, while sitting on the end of a bed in a vacant suite, intuition told her something was amiss. She scanned the space again and everything seemed tip-top—it was a comfortable, luxurious suite. Then, to her horror, she noticed that the colourful watercolours of hibiscus, birds of paradise and bougainvillea had vanished from their mahogany frames. Aghast, she stared in disbelief. Each of the six frames now held a highly explicit page torn from *Hustler* magazine. The scariest part, she told me, was that the pornographic pictures could have been there since she'd last inspected the room. No guest or member of the staff had said a word.

Our first retreat week of the year flew by. The guests have just departed, after hugging us and each other like fourteen-year-olds on the last day of camp, with email addresses exchanged, promises made to connect when they get back home, and tears shared. All of them looked ten years younger than when they arrived, all now excited for their own next chapters.

We have all survived the usual dramas, a sure thing when you mix wine and women sharing stories and meeting future friends. Stuff will happen.

For instance, once, just after Jacky and I had given each other a high-five because the group seemed fabulous, Georgia from Calgary stumbled into the kitchen. "I have seen a bee!" she cried, white-faced.

Confused, we asked what the problem was.

"I am highly allergic. There was absolutely no mention in the information package about there being bees in Italy, so I did not bring my EpiPen."

Then there were the mother and daughter who seemed to be having relationship problems, dis- covered by Luca early one morning asleep by the pool, alongside numerous empty wine bot- tles. What that was about we never found out.

I also remember a scary moment involving a guest, a wasp and a sandwich, and another woman who discovered a scorpion dozing within a pair of folded pyjamas.

But this week there have been no calamities. An uneventful week at the retreat always means a successful one.

I am knackered when the group leaves, mostly due to the barrage of questions I'm always asked about life in Italy. Our guests are rightly fascinated about what it takes to move here, and after a week here, they are usually wondering if they can follow in our footsteps.

I answer as best I can.

Does one need an EU passport? *No.*

Can one buy a house in joint names? *Yes.*

Is it challenging to find a good builder? *No.*

Did you ever want to give up? *Yes, all the time.*

How bad is the bureaucracy?

And with my answer to this question, I dampen their enthusiasm forever, destroying any romantic thoughts they might have had about running home to their partner, announcing, "We are moving to Tuscany."

The story I tell them is just one example of the horrors you need to withstand to buy a place in this highly protected region of the country and renovate it. I came seriously close to pulling my hair out, along with what was left of our architect Umberto's mop. During the renovation years, he and I waited many a month for Signora Bertelli in the *municipio* (the local town hall) to stamp our much-needed building permits, even though we'd received permission for the work from her superiors in the permit office in Siena, often months before. On one occasion I remember,

Umberto and I stood in front of her desk like children being told off in the headmaster's office while she impatiently told us that she needed to send our paperwork to yet another colleague, delaying us by a month.

"Where is this person's office?" I asked.

She pointed through her open door to another door across the hallway. "Signore Colombo is a very busy man. I will send the papers to him soon, and when he has signed them, you will be able to start the work."

"He's over in that office?" I growled.

She nodded.

Furious, I picked up the papers and stormed out of her office and into Signore Colombo's across the hall. "Please sign!"

He glanced at the papers and signed.

I had won this particular battle, but there were more permits to go—twenty-eight, in fact.

By the time I reach the end of this story, I can see that the guests have already changed their plans—a vacation home in Florida sounds lovely.

# Summer

"In the summertime, when the weather is hot,
you can stretch right up and touch the sky."

—MUNGO JERRY

# You Clean Up Well!

A sense of humour and tremendous staying power is essential to survive the summer in Tuscany. A healthy liver helps too.

The tourists flood the Renaissance cities of Florence, Venice and the historic capital, Rome. Holiday homeowners return from every corner of the globe, flinging open shutters and cleaning out whatever has nested in the pizza oven while they've been gone. Then the expats who now call Tuscany home leap into summer's social whirl with the enthusiasm of kids let out of school. The Italians, too, embrace the season with gusto. They flee their cramped city apartments and head to the hills, mountains and beaches of their own glorious country. Everywhere people dance to a frenzied rhythm of festivals, parties, open-air concerts, theatre and nightly *aperitivi*. Summer here can bring you to your knees.

When we first arrived, we soon became the flavour of the month for the Tuscan expat community, always on the lookout for fresh meat. We were invited to every event: summer soirees, concerts on a castle's grounds, picturesque vineyard picnics, fancy dinner parties. I am not complaining—it was an enticing, exciting way to meet people. It was also an eye-opener, a lesson that clarified why we had taken on this rural life.

At one fancy affair in Chianti, an area popular with well-off Brits, an elderly Englishman left me open-mouthed when he explained to me in posh Queen's English (as if talking with a mouthful of plums), "The summer here is painfully dreadful. There are way too many foreigners for my liking!" Pretty absurd when he was part of the influx that caused this region of Tuscany to be nicknamed "Chiantishire." South of Chianti, in the Val d'Orcia, where we live, for now the locals still outnumber the foreigners.

As the years passed, we were inevitably dethroned by the new "it" couple and the invitations dwindled. Still, I don't regret that initial crazy social whirl. Whenever I move to a new place, I try to be open to meeting as many people as possible; even if they aren't my cup of tea, I always find others who are. My friends here are a mixed crowd, replanted in the Tuscan countryside from a variety of places. These are the people who have helped shape the journey we have chosen in our adopted land. We *stranieri* all have one thing in common: a mutual love and appreciation for this enchanting place. And though we will always be foreigners to them, the Tuscans have been kind and welcoming; they, too, have helped us build a life here.

I have been lucky to befriend some interesting souls. There are the talented New Yorkers Wendy and John, who live in the turret of the medieval castle up the hill from us. They are a movie industry couple—a music composer and a lighting director who fly back and forth over the pond like others take the bus. As we sip coffee in the village bar, amongst farmers who are probably discussing the merits of different fertilizers, Wendy shares tales of being at the Oscars and the Tribeca Film Festival.

Then there are our British friends, high-powered litigation lawyers from London who strip off their business suits the minute they arrive and throw themselves into working the land around their small farmhouse. And my Canadian pal who, straight after an acrimonious divorce twenty years ago, came here alone on holiday, bought an apartment in a restored monastery and started a new life on a whim and a wisp.

Our friendships have blossomed quickly out of necessity. We assist each other with handling the arduous Italian bureaucracy and join forces over countless chores on our respective hunks of land. The fact that you held down a brilliant job for decades really doesn't matter when there are grapes to be picked, olives to be pressed and trees to trim. We spend most days dressed in shabby work clothes. So when we meet up at some fancy evening event, we often shake our heads in surprise and blurt out things like "Well, you clean up well!"

My first friend in Tuscany was the highly successful author Frances Mayes. I reached out to her because *Entertainment Tonight* was filming a segment about me jumping from the television world into running retreats, and I wanted to interview Frances; her bestselling book *Under the Tuscan Sun* had been my inspiration to restore a crumbling farmhouse. She agreed, and soon we were on camera, chatting about the wonders and the challenges of renovating overseas. It turned into so much more than an interview. Frances is an encyclopedia of everyday life in Italy. Not only did she guide us in the art of restoration, but she also helped us navigate the summer social scene. Best of all, we became firm friends.

There was one evening we spent with Frances and her husband, Ed, that I will never forget. Jeremy Irons, the Oscar-, Emmy- and Tony-award-winning actor, had agreed to take on the theatrical role of Frédéric Chopin, appearing opposite Sharon Stone (Hans's favourite Hollywood icon—not sure why) as Chopin's long-time lover George Sand. The play featured them reading the letters the lovers had written back and forth to each other during the turbulent last years of Chopin's life. Between each letter, a pianist would play the composer's music. The performance was to be staged in the Teatro Signorelli, a magnificent theatre in the middle of Cortona, as part of the Tuscan Sun Festival, which Frances had founded.

At the last moment, Stone had to bail and was replaced by the talented Irish actress Sinéad Cusack, Irons's wife. Hans may have been disappointed, but it was a glamorous night. He and I walked the red carpet alongside the likes of Greta Scacchi, Sting and Trudie Styler. Thanks to Frances, we had front-row seats in a theatre that is a neoclassical wonder of vaulted ceilings, lush red seats and romantic boxes. As we found our places, we looked up to see that the stage was set simply, just two high-backed wing chairs placed on either side of a grand piano.

We all applauded enthusiastically as Irons and Cusack entered. As they sat, the audience settled, and Mr. Irons began reading the first letter in his deep, penetrating voice. As he finished, everyone clapped again, but then the eminent pianist made his entrance and the applause turned into an explosion of sound, with some wolf whistles from the cheap seats too. I am a philistine when it comes to classical music, and I have to admit I might have been the only one who had no idea who the pianist was (I still don't).

Dressed in black tails, white gloves and a silk scarf, he bowed towards the thrilled spectators, who in turn leaned towards him in awe. The crowd seemed to hold its breath as he removed his gloves and scarf and laid them beside him on the piano bench. He glanced from the audience to the actors, and then he sat and began to play, bathing us in Chopin's music. Even I was mesmerized by the beauty and sensitivity of his work.

He had been playing for less than two minutes when, from the direction of one of the theatre boxes above the stage,

a cellphone began to ring, blaring Metallica through the theatre. We heard a chair crashing to the floor as the terrified owner of the phone rummaged for it. The pianist waited with his hands frozen above the keys. As Mr. Irons and Ms. Cusack glared up at the cellphone sinner, we all stared at our knees, hoping no one would think we were the ones responsible for this atrocity, and very thankful we weren't guilty.

Finally, the phone stopped ringing. Lowering his hands to the keys, the pianist played on, but not for long. Thirty seconds later, the same raucous racket resounded throughout the theatre from the repeat offender.

At that, the pianist slammed the piano's lid shut, grabbed his gloves, flung the white silk scarf around his neck and, with his head held high, left the stage. The grim actors followed.

Frances leaned towards me and whispered, "Early dinner, I suppose!"


Thankfully, that disastrous evening was not my fault. But last year I experienced my own red-faced moment. Hans and I had been invited to a fourteenth-century convent recently restored as a jaw-dropping private home. The hosts were a Belgian couple we'd befriended as we simultaneously renovated our Tuscan ruins. We'd met over a pile of stone slabs in a recycling yard and bonded over our passion for restoration projects. My television shows were airing in Belgium at the time, and I became a sought-after guest at their parties.

Already renowned for holding glamorous soirees, our hosts had outdone themselves. Flickering flames from antique torches guided us down a garden path towards a gathering of impeccably dressed guests mingling and chatting in a slew of different languages. I was tempted to grab my phone and capture the breathtaking setting, but decided this was not a crowd that appreciated social media. The sun had sunk behind a copse of cypress trees by the time we all gathered for an alfresco dinner at a long table where candelabra shimmered over vases of wild poppies and crystal wineglasses.

At the table for what was sure to be a meal fit for a king, I glanced over at Hans, who was separated from me, happy amongst a bevy of beauties. I had a prime seat between two gentlemen. One was an Italian winemaker of much authority, or so he said; the other I had yet to meet. As we tucked into skinny baby asparagus with freshly shaved truffle, I turned my attention from the winemaker to the bloke on my other side.

"Hello, I'm Debbie Travis. Lovely to meet you," I said. I reached for the first icebreaker I could think of, politely inquiring, "What do you do?"

"I am the king of Belgium," he said, smiling.

"Ha, and I am the queen of England," I guffawed, adding a friendly thump to his bicep.

We spent the next twenty minutes enjoying each other's company. I told him about a burst sewage pipe that had recently flooded our kitchen, and he shared a story about a delightful trip to an opera held in a Greek amphitheatre.

After we finished the *primo*, a delicate ravioli stuffed with ricotta and sage, as the plates were being removed, I excused myself to go to the loo. On the way, I bumped into our hostess.

"You look as if you are having fun with our honoured guest, his majesty, the king of Belgium," she said.

My first dinner with royalty and I blew it.

Although I once spent an hour with Sarah Ferguson, the duchess of York, who herself would admit to blowing it far more times than I had. We were both speaking at a women's event at the Convention Centre in Toronto. I have waited in more green rooms than most people have had hot dinners, but this time I was the only non-royal in the room. The others waiting their turn to enlighten the vast audience with Fergie and me were Queen Noor of Jordan and the most flamboyant queen of them all, the exercise guru Richard Simmons.

"Let's liven up this room," he commanded, tossing his tightly permed head of curls. Dressed in his famous satin cut-off shorts and sequined tank top, he leapt from the back of the sofa onto the coffee table.

His laughter and energy were so contagious, the queen, the duchess and I all joined him for a wild, disco-inspired workout minutes before we hit the stage.

Throughout the summer, the invitations keep on coming. We meet up with friends for alfresco lunches in nearby piazzas, fooling ourselves that we are on holiday like the surrounding tourists. We discuss rumours about the declining flocks of sheep in the valley, farmers unable to compete with the price of the milk being trucked in from Switzerland to produce the local pecorino cheese. For some reason, the next generation of farm children find no glamour in a career as a shepherd. "So sad, kids today!" we lament.

"Did you hear that Geoffrey Rush has bought a place outside the village? I loved him in *The King's Speech*."

"Wish it was Colin Firth! I would definitely invite him over for a glass of something."

With guilty grins, we agree to yet another bottle of Chianti, attempting to blot out the nagging list of chores and Zoom calls waiting for us back home. Hooky is such a delight when it involves a lazy afternoon in good company, copious glasses of *vino* and a simple Tuscan meal.

Today there is no restaurant lunch for me. I am knuckled down, preparing for the first classic car rally of the year, which will take place in a week's time. Still, with Hans away, if I get all my work done, I'll head solo to an *aperitivo* I've been invited to; even though it's just drinks and nibbles, it promises to be a swanky affair. I actually prefer this Italian custom to a sit-down dinner, which usually starts late and ends in the wee hours. At an *aperitivo*, you can have an evening out and a catch-up with friends and yet be happily tucked up in bed by ten.

When I finish my chores, I get myself cleaned up and pull out my poshest dress, a Stella McCartney bargain I found on sale years ago. It's my go-to ensemble when I know the other guests will be decked out in the latest designer outfits.

I've met the host, a guru in the world of high fashion, but this is my first opportunity to visit his home. Knowing that mutual friends have also been invited, I head out alone to his sprawling country pile. I arrive at an apricot-coloured villa, apparently built in the fifteenth century by a member of the Medici family for his mistress. Lucky lady. I ring a monster door pull. The door is opened by a butler, and not just any penguin-suited butler, but a dazzling Sikh wearing a ruby-coloured turban, a turquoise uniform and matching slippers threaded with gold.

I step into the pages of *Elle Decor*, featuring candlelit rooms decorated in my favourite style: bohemian chic. The sound of a cellist playing on a terrace fills the perfumed air. The partygoers are just as elegantly dressed as I anticipated, bejewelled in vintage Bulgari. After I am introduced around by our host, I follow a woman I've met before into the kitchen. She owns a landscaping company in Milan, and I'm keen to pick her brain about the succulents I am planning to plant in the garden this year. As I unleash a barrage of questions, she kindly pulls two stools close to a kitchen island created from two gigantic chestnut beams. Spritzes in hand, we chat. A plate of miniature carrots sits in front of us, and I munch as I soak up valuable planting tips. The carrots are a little ugly, and they taste strange, but they go down okay with the booze. Hungry and missing out on the plates of bruschetta and platters of pecorino cheese that are being passed around the living room, I crunch through three or four of the little things. Then I thank her for her help and we join the throng. Three hours later, I'm home.

*What a pleasant evening*, I think while cleaning my face. I look up, smiling, into the mirror. Horrified, I stare at my fluorescent-orange lips and terracotta-stained teeth. No one at the party said a thing, too polite to mention that the "carrots" I'd grazed on were turmeric roots.

It takes three days and a full tube of toothpaste mixed with lemon juice to get my pearly whites back. It is imperative that both my smile and the property are in perfect shape for the classic car rally.

—

Several years ago, friends invited us to join them on what would turn out to be a transformative trip. We were two couples within a group of thirty people from around the world who set off to discover France and Italy from behind the wheels of classic cars supplied by a museum in Munich, Germany.

The route took us from Nice, in the south of France, along back roads to Lake Como, in northern Italy. We wound our way through hillside villages, alongside miles of rice paddies and around two of Italy's great lakes, Maggiore and Como. Hans was in heaven, driving a Bugatti built in the 1930s. Pedestrians waved from the roadside and cars honked their appreciation as we went by. Cars from a bygone era evoke wonder and joy, not envy, in most people, thanks to their sexy curves, racing colours and throaty engines.

I sat in the passenger seat, my mind racing faster than the car. There was an opportunity here. Villa Reniella was the ideal location to hold a car rally. Drive east through Umbria's forested mountains and wide, lush valleys, or head west and be immersed in the heart of the Tuscan landscape. Motor north through miles of Chianti vineyards, or southwest, where the hills slope towards the Mediterranean Sea like fingers stretching out to greet the coast. Any direction a rally took from the villa would be breathtaking. Before we had completed the three-day adventure with our friends, I had created a plan to hold our own rallies. We needed cars and mechanics, of course, and soon found both when mutual friends introduced us to the handsome Frenchman Fabien.

Jump ahead three years and here we are, on the eve of our sixth classic car rally. Twenty-four guests will arrive in the morning. The precious cargo of classic cars has been unloaded from flatbed trucks and carefully driven down the newly groomed and extremely steep gravel driveway. The villagers, along with every young lad

from miles around, came to watch the scene. Hans, too, back from his short trip away (thankfully unaware that my smile was recently tangerine-coloured).

Tonight, the air is thick and warm, and we take advantage of the last evening of peace to slip into the cool pool. A rare time together, just us and the stars. In the far distance, we see a streak of silver, followed by a whisper of thunder. Too far away to be of any concern, we think—someone else's storm. Two hours later, our driveway has been washed away in a Biblical downpour that departed as quickly as it arrived.

Up at the crack of dawn, only hours before the guests invade, Hans frantically works the phone. Paolo, the gentle giant who rescued the pond, saves the day again, resurfacing the entire kilometre-long driveway to perfection within hours of the rally kickoff.

Expectations realized, the guests circle the proud fleet parked in a shimmering circle of gleaming metal, their wide smiles saying it all. A cheeky silver Porsche 911 Targa with a turquoise leather interior, a metallic-bronze Rolls-Royce from the 1960s, an Alfa Romeo that has appeared in numerous movies, a naughty red Ferrari and a Mercedes convertible once owned by Patrick Duffy, the actor from *Dallas*—these are just a few of the collection, each beauty with a story to tell. With the devotion of new mothers, the mechanics explain the workings of the cars, what buttons to press and, more importantly, what not to touch. And then, with a final roar, our guests are off.

I am only halfway through my first cappuccino when Hans calls. George, a guest from Florida, pulled a knob on the dashboard of the tomato-coloured 1965 Jaguar E-Type—a knob he was told not to touch. The extremely long hood, renowned in this model, flew up, blocking his view of the road. Screeching to an emergency "blind" stop, he slid into a utility pole rudely standing in his way. Neither the driver nor the passenger is hurt, which is a relief, but the car is badly dinged up. And, Hans tells me, Fabien is behind a bush, sobbing over his hurt baby. Soon, he and the mechanics load the battered car onto the truck we sent to follow the group, a new one is brought forward, and off George goes again. Apart from the occasional wrong turn into farmyards and one couple who get lost for a few hours, the rest of the four-day rally is a magnificent success.

Fabien has, thankfully, stopped crying.

"Love is just a word until someone
comes along and gives it meaning."
—PAULO COELHO

# And They Called It Puppy Love

I was a just a girl when Donny Osmond's megahit "Puppy Love" was blasting the airwaves day and night, sending legions of teenage girls into ecstasy. I was so young I didn't realize that he was singing about a boy and a girl. I thought the song really was about a puppy. Who wouldn't love a puppy madly? I, too, wanted a puppy, but my pleading fell on my mother's deaf ears.

When our boys were young, our lives were too hectic to take on responsibility for any pet more demanding than a goldfish. But then came Alfie, and so today we are heading to Rome to meet the nine-week-old border collie that Fabrizio, the breeder, has picked out for us from the new litter sired by the same champion that was Alfie's father, guaranteeing that the puppy will be both handsome and good-tempered.

Still, for the entire two-hour journey, I enumerate the pros and cons of doing this again. Hans drives, stone-faced, as I run through every scenario I can think of when it comes to taking on another dog. We still feel such guilt and sadness—is it too soon

after the trauma of Alfie's accident? Can we cope with the early mornings, toys scattered everywhere in the house and losing the freedom to travel on a whim? By the time we reach the eternal city, I've exhausted us both. We head along the perfectly straight roads bordered by *Pinus pinea* that stretch from Rome to the coast. Normally, I would be hanging out the window, filming these majestic lines of flat-topped trees, but I am too deep in thought.

Hans attempts to relieve the tension by saying, "Did you know it was the dictator Mussolini who planted these avenues of umbrella trees?"

"Hmm," I say. "But what if we can't love the new puppy as much as we loved Alfie?"

"Let's wait until we get there. If it doesn't feel right, we will return home empty-handed," he says kindly.

We meet the puppies in Fabrizio's garden. A metal playpen sits in the shade of a large olive tree with what look like five miniature pandas tumbling over each other inside of it. From the middle of the pile of black-and-white fur, a cheeky face pops up and looks straight at us. Fabrizio smiles and points at the culprit.

He is the smallest in the litter, but he's holding his own in the boisterous bundle. There's a white star on his forehead. He has three white legs and one black one with a white paw, as if he's a schoolboy with a sock around his ankle, and he wears the trademark white fur shirt front of the show line border collie on his chest. The puppy bounces towards us as if he knows we are his future. When Hans picks him up, he is rewarded with the sweetest puppy kiss. Cradling the dog, Hans turns to me and says, "Let's go home."

On the drive back, our grown-up sons call. "Well, did you get him?"

When we tell them yes, they excitedly suggest names for him from their childhood: Bert or Ernie, Ninja or Batman.

I sit in the back seat, holding the wide-eyed pup, who's taking it all in. "I would like to call him Billie," I announce to the three men in my life. "He's sweet-natured and funny, and he is so handsome. He reminds me of my father."

My dad's name was Bill, but my mother called him Billie. He was my childhood happiness. I was twelve when he died. My life changed the day he left, but his soul has been forever by my side.

Hans says, "Billie it is."

"Mad dogs and Englishmen go out in the midday sun . . ."

—NOEL COWARD

# The Sweetness
# of Doing Nothing

So far this year we have waved off one wellness group, a girls' getaway, a gourmet cooking event and two classic car rallies. Now we get to take a break.

Others may picture a perfect summer as time spent lounging on a dock at a cottage overlooking a wild lake surrounded by towering pines, or dozing through lazy picnics in the park, or sailing the high seas in a steady wind. Whatever floats your boat. But for me, the epitome of summer is Tuscany, when the countryside is at its peak and the entire spectrum of summer sensations surrounds us. All is in full bloom, the garden luminous. The fragrance of wild thyme, mint and fennel waft around us as we walk the land. Clumps of purple lavender kiss our bare legs, releasing perfumed clouds. Climbing jasmine, so unassuming during the day, delights us as the sun disappears, filling the evening air with its sweet aroma.

Summer sounds different from the rest of the year. The dry earth and parched grass crackling underfoot. A splash, followed by laughter. The muffled chatter of Hans and my younger son discussing whatever fathers and sons talk about. A creak from the hammock. The swish of the pages turning in a book meant only to be entertaining, interrupted by the pop of a wine cork. As the temperature soars, the cicadas' deafening song underpins the summer harmony.

We live in floppy hats and long, floaty dresses. (Hans looks marvellous in his.) The new puppy bounces around on his journey of discovery, periodically cooling off under an olive tree. For man and beast, the only stress is finding shade and avoiding getting the pages of your book soaked when friends leap into the pool.

*Dolce far niente* has become an Instagram theme that can mean anything from enjoying being lazy to appreciating the moment as one is meant to do in mindful meditation. But for me, the Italian idiom is all about embracing the art of just *being*, which I excel at. I spend many days in July and August flip-flopping from pool to hammock, kitchen to vegetable garden, with Billie trailing me. He revels in leaping into the raised wooden beds, low enough for a four-month-old puppy to manage, where he disappears amongst the lettuce and uproots the green beans.

The *orto* feeds us and our guests a wide variety of vegetables. Like the entire population of Italy, we eat only what is in season. It sounds lovely as an idea, but I admit it can become tedious. Peas and fava beans are on almost every menu throughout May. June signals the beginning of an endless run of string beans. By July, the *orto* is a battleground of foaming tomato plants and out-of-control zucchini. Some of the zucchini tendrils spiral up the old olive tree that sits on the edge of the garden, and soon zucchini the size of limbs hang from the branches, a source of hilarity for all.

A bonanza of tomatoes is never a problem. I bottle and freeze the bounty into sauces and soups that will see us through to the following tomato season. But I cannot pick the zucchini fast enough. Left to their own devices, they will monopolize the garden like Jack's magic beanstalk. One day I will wake up to find zucchini tendrils climbing through the bedroom window and wrapping themselves around me and my sleeping spouse.

Before we are completely invaded, I settle beside the pool with a pile of cookbooks, in search of recipes. It is hard to concentrate, though. Like clockwork, the swifts are paying their late-afternoon visit. Whirling high above me, they own the sky. Then they swoop, dive-bombing the pool, gracefully skimming the surface for insects and sips of water until their internal timer goes off and they disappear, probably to a neighbouring pool over the valley.

I stare up at the villa above me and watch it turn from buttery yellow to the colour of toast as the ancient stone walls soak up the late-afternoon sun. I rarely look back on the journey that brought us here or the body of work that allowed Hans and me to create this haven, but this is one of those pinch-me-I'm-dreaming moments.

I close my eyes and allow my mind to wander back to my childhood home, a suburban house in Rochdale, Lancashire, that my parents had built themselves. Most of the homes in the area were in rows of terraced houses nicknamed "one up, one down"— one room on the ground floor and one room upstairs. No bathroom; the privy was at the bottom of a narrow backyard. Our house was a mock Tudor with five bedrooms and an inside bathroom, a comfortable family home big enough to accommodate lodgers after my dad died.

In my late teens and early twenties, I moved on to a series of beloved hovels in London, a far cry from where I am now. My first flatmate, Mandy (whose name I've changed as she may not be as willing as I am to share our survival strategy), and I earned just enough money from our start-up modelling careers to pay our meagre rent. To eat, we relied on a slew of hopeful guys who took us out for dinner. We often stuffed bread rolls into our underwear for the next day's breakfast. Even so, the thrill of being independent—out on our own and away from parental supervision—outweighed the dodgy London lodgings. In the first basement bedsit Mandy and I shared, my bedroom was the broom cupboard under the stairs, which was the width of a single mattress. We graduated to a grand flat with four bedrooms shared by twelve partygoers. It does not take a math genius to work out the chaotic sleeping arrangements.

Realtors prattle on about the importance of "location, location, location." With my third rental, I achieved just that: 27 Sloane Gardens, right off the expensively chic Sloane Square in Chelsea. By this time Mandy had run off to work the beach bars of Majorca and I'd hooked up with a new buddy, Julia (best to change her name too). Through sheer bravado and low-cut T-shirts, we managed to secure a flat in one of Sloane Gardens' five-storey, red-brick Victorians, which had once been a fancy private home. How could two struggling models afford the rent? Granny to the rescue. After I told Joyce I was in desperate need of a new abode, she contacted Dickie, who owned one of these houses. A bloke she'd befriended in a previous life, Dickie was obviously still infatuated with her and, after we met with him in those flashy T-shirts, he agreed to lease the tiny flat in the basement to us at a pathetically low rent. We had lucked out. We were a minute from the Tube and on the edge of the outrageous King's Road, the birthplace of the miniskirt, home to punk rock, edgy art galleries and notorious wine bars.

Chelsea was the place to be, and still is. But the massive terraced house we'd moved into was far removed from the brightly coloured, bustling neighbourhood. Stone stairs climbed up from the tree-lined street to a once-imposing entrance. The huge door, its green paint chipped and its brass knocker tarnished, had seen better days. The cavernous entrance hall was dank, dark and dingy, with flocked maroon wallpaper, threadbare carpets and dusty chandeliers. If you dared to stop and look around, you would be startled by displays of dusty stuffed birds that must have kept a taxidermist in full-time employment for years. Dickie had divided the once-opulent family home into flats a decade earlier, each with its own heavy mahogany door. We fantasized about who lived behind each one, but as we soon discovered, no one else lived there but old Dickie, who inhabited a huge apartment on the second floor. It turned out our landlord, an only child, had been born in the grand house. Property rich but cash poor after his parents died, he'd converted the place into apartments so he could afford to stay on, but he'd then let them fall into such disrepair that they now sat empty.

Dickie, who struck us as creepy but harmless, occasionally materialized from behind a giant rubber plant in the hallway or slithered into our flat to check the electric meter, leaving behind a rancid whiff of fried food and unwashed socks. His shiny comb-over—six greasy strands of hair—and his waxy skin, the colour of five-day-old chicken, sent shudders through our young bodies. Very occasionally we would join him over a cuppa and biscuits and listen to his stories of a life less lonely.

We stayed at Sloane Gardens for two years, busy with the stuff that young women fill their days and nights with and mostly disinterested in anything but ourselves. Then Julia arrived home one day to say there was a dreadful odour in the entrance hall. With nervous giggles, we followed the smell up the staircase to Dickie's doorway. We knocked. No answer. Julia, the braver of the two of us, checked the door, which was unlocked, crept into his flat and found him in bed, departed from this world, surrounded by stuffed birds. How long he had lain there undiscovered, and why he'd surrounded himself with dead birds, we never found out. After we called the police, we moved out, retreating to Julia's parents' house on the east coast of England. We were bored and broke and not terribly happy on our blow-up mattresses, with no idea what to do next. Then, to our utter surprise, we found out that Dickie had left us a little something in his will. Two thousand pounds each, to be exact.

With this, we rented our first decent flat. I still bless Dickie.

> "Italians are entirely without any commitment to order.
> They live their lives in a kind of pandemonium,
> which I find very attractive."
>
> —BILL BRYSON

# Please Stay Home!

This is a severe but well-meant advisory: do not, under any circumstances, come to Italy in August, especially if your idea of a holiday is wandering peacefully through the countryside by car, relaxing in a piazza sipping a cappuccino and watching the locals go about their day-to-day routine, or, God forbid, lounging on the beach. If it is August, don't come!  Either go somewhere else in the world or stay home.

Ferragosto is the annual national holiday that officially starts on August 15. But as is the way in Italy, the nation begins to wind down a week or so earlier to give people time to pack and prepare for the frenzy of a non-stop *festa*. The same goes for the end of Ferragosto. Businesses are supposed to reopen by the end of the month, but it can be October before normality reigns.

At the villa, we spend the first week of August finishing any jobs that can't wait a month. Today, Massi, Christian and Luca are stripped to the waist, checking the irrigation system; with water precious after two months with no rain, we've dialled it down to a trickle.

There is a builder on the roof of the barn, repairing loose tiles, naked save for what looks like a cloth diaper, similar to the ones in the drawings of the Egyptians building the pyramids. This is not an unusual sight in Tuscany in the summer, though I will never get used to chatting to tradesmen swaddled in baggy nappies that only precariously hold in their dangly bits. When they shout down a question from the roof and I look up, nothing is left to the imagination!

These builders and landscapers have worked here since the renovation began over ten years ago and, apart from the language challenges, we all get on well and appreciate each other's cultures. But as a foreigner it is impossible for me to understand the summer vacation antics in Italy. Believe me, I love a beach holiday as much as any Italian, but not Italian beaches in the month of August.

Imagine for a moment the magnificent long, sandy shores of Cape Cod, on the east coast of the United States. I often took my family there when the boys were young. We would drag our paraphernalia—picnic blankets, folding chairs, food baskets and bags of swimming stuff—to the quietest spot, no matter how far it was from the parking lot. My aim was to find a deserted area far away from other beachgoers so it would feel like we had the place to ourselves.

But that is not the goal of Italians on summer vacation, oh no! All Italian beaches are public beaches, but some are more public than others. The protected national parks are stunning and usually empty, featuring endless stretches of sand with no amenities—no restaurants, burger bars or loos. But why would any fun-loving Italian want to be alone on a picturesque sandy beach when they could be crammed like a tinned sardine head-to-toe with their neighbours, co-workers, friends and family? As far as I can tell, Italians prefer to travel in packs.

Most of the public beaches are managed by beach clubs— hundreds of them. Feel free to walk along the water's edge, but never attempt to park yourself on one of the tightly packed sun loungers that lie under rows of multicoloured parasols. They may be empty, but beware: they'll have been reserved by families for *generations*. If you aren't a member of a beach club, you will be offered costly loungers to rent, usually beside the toilets and over-flowing garbage bins. A trip to the Maldives can be less expensive.

If you have ever visited the popular Cinque Terre on the Ligurian Riviera, five brightly coloured fishing villages precar-iously nestled between cliffs and the Mediterranean Sea, you'll know there is the odd slice of sand around but there are no real beaches. Here, the imperative is the same in terms of bodies per square inch, but the holidaymakers have to turn into contortion-ists. Cramming themselves onto the giant boulders that line the shore, they spread out towels and soak up the sun until, like lem-mings, they head off en masse to ear-splittingly noisy quayside restaurants for three-hour-long lunches. This level of madness can be found along the shores of the entire peninsula of Italy during the extreme heat of August.

Mind you, good-natured Italians are not the only ones head-ing to the coast. The roads are bumper to bumper with camper vans, flocks of motorbikes, family sedans and convertibles with number plates from across Europe and Britain, an exodus of increasingly distraught dads, hysterical mothers and whinging kids caught in an eternal traffic jam. Engines overheat; tempers erupt. We, too, attempted one of these holidays. I very nearly murdered one (maybe two) of my own after one of our young lads reached through from the back seat of the car and rubbed gum through my hair as the other monster (yes, you know who you are) plonked a paper bag with a soggy sandwich still inside it over his father's head whilst we were speeding down the autoroute.

Let's say you ignored my warnings and survived the stressful journey to an Italian beach in August. Fantastic! Now's the time to grab the towels, the picnic basket and the toys for the kids. But there is a strict dress code on Italian beaches. Here are the rules on what and what not to wear:

1. All adults, in sea and on sand, must wear bottoms except on designated nudist beaches.
2. Babies and toddlers can run around naked.
3. Topless? No problem. Oh, except in restaurants, where tops *and* bottoms are mandatory.
4. Pensioners must wear the skimpiest of bathing suits.
5. An average bloke may prefer board shorts or boxer-style swimwear, but on Italian beaches you will still see many overly tanned men, wrinkled as prunes, parading in tiny grape smugglers, nut huts, budgie smugglers, scrote totes or truffle duffels. These are just a few of the evocative names for the thongs and Speedos still popular on European beaches.

So Hans and I have learned to stay home and away from the beach in August, even though, when we try to go for a walk, the punishing heat hits like a blow to the head and the only relief is a mad dash to the pool. I'm usually the only mad fool heading outside. The puppy and the hubby prefer lying spread-eagled on the villa's heavenly cold stone floors. The countryside around us is stunned into silence, the only sound being the high-pitched buzz of cicadas in the olive trees. The empty village streets ripple in a haze of heat, shutters closed against the unforgiving sun.

But even in these hottest weeks, I love my Tuscan home— and so do all my friends. In July and August, the villa becomes an informal open house to a mix of travellers, long-time and newfound chums alongside our sons, their wives and their friends. I spend my days frying eggs and washing sheets. The turn-over is epic.

Our friends usually arrive with lists of restaurants to try, daylong hikes mapped out, and plans for bike rides through the hills of Tuscany and trips to taste the wines at a huge selection of vineyards, not to mention visits to the plethora of museums and churches. But when they experience the tranquilizing effect of their first afternoon by the pool, all their well-laid plans go out the window. I can't count the number of times I've heard something like this: "It's so relaxing here! Would it be okay if we just take in the view and chill? Well, yes, a glass of wine would be lovely, thank you, but please don't go to any trouble. A light lunch, you say? Sure, we'd be up for that."

When a well-known television host came to stay a few years ago, she asked me to create a list of things to do. When she arrived, I handed her a printed itinerary. She took one look at the hammock and tore up the list, and from that moment on, she barely moved from her chosen spot. We spent a marvellous week putting the world to rights over copious glasses of Aperol spritz.

I hasten to add that this is all fine with me, so long as our friends and family take turns loading the exhausted dishwasher. But we *have* had to set some house rules:

1. **Bring a car.** "Oh, please don't worry, we'll grab an Uber." Very funny. There are no Ubers here. No taxis, either, and the local donkey has retired. And you can't count on the occasional, highly unreliable bus. Guests need their own transport.
2. **Stay no more than five days.** A visit of five days means guests leave on a high note, without me murdering anyone and burying them in the *bosco*. (If you care to look, you'll find several bodies under the oak trees in the woods.)

3.  Please **fill your rental car with bottles of booze before you come**; none of it will go to waste here.

4.  **Do not bring your dirty laundry**; we are not a launderette. My biggest peeve is someone who arrives and informs us, "Sorry, but we've been travelling for weeks and the laundry service at the hotel in Rome was ridiculously expensive, so we would be grateful if you could wash a few items. Johnny, bring the suitcases."

5.  **Leave your room tidy when you depart.** This means throwing out the carrier bags from all that shopping you enjoyed, rather than leaving them scattered over the floor. And bring those empty wine bottles and coffee cups back to the kitchen. (To be fair, I used to leave hotel rooms looking like a tornado had hit them. If, by any chance, a housekeeper from a hotel I have stayed at is reading this, I apologize for my mess. After running our place, I am a changed person.)

6.  **If you decide to set off for a walk** along one of the numerous trails through the woods and over yonder, please **let us know before you leave**. There have been many meals where we've suddenly discovered that someone is missing.
    "What happened to Jane and John?"
    "Oh, I saw them wandering down by the pond at dawn."
    "Their dinner is getting cold—I wonder if they're lost."
    Inevitably they are, and a search party needs to head out while everyone else's food also gets cold.

One rule I've made for myself: be wary of messages from people we haven't heard from in years that go something like this.

*Hey, how are you? It's me, Michelle. Remember we worked together at the network years ago? Gosh, it has been ages since we saw you—must be a dozen years. Congratulations on your beautiful place in Tuscany. I follow you on social media. Looks amazing. Hey, do you remember our little Amanda? She was six months old when you last saw her. She's all grown up now and presently backpacking across Europe with friends. She would love to see you again and was wondering if she could pop in for a month. Wouldn't that be awesome?*

Being a public figure is a privilege, and I find it heartwarming to meet viewers and followers. But when they drop by unannounced, it can be uncomfortable.

Though we have no gate, it's obvious that the villa is a private property. One Sunday afternoon, I was out walking in the lower olive grove when I heard chatting. I headed towards the source and found a family settled in around our pool.

"Hey there!" the man hailed me in a thick Texan accent. "How ya doing?"

"I am doing fine, thank you," I said, remaining calm. "Can I help you?"

"My wife here, Betsy Boo, follows you on Instagram, so we came for a look around. These are our two kids."

"Sounds like you're from Texas?"

"We are—we're from Houston."

"Tell me," I said, "if I walked into your garden and sat by your pool, you would probably shoot me. Is that correct?"

They got the point and soon left, mumbling about my rudeness.

Just a few weeks ago, as Hans and I basked in our first weekend alone for quite a while, I was stripping off to jump into the pool in my birthday suit when an Australian couple and their limousine driver appeared around the corner of the villa. I grabbed a tablecloth that was hanging from the nearby washing line. (A split second later and I would have been naked. That would have scared them off.)

The couple told me they were staying in Siena, forty minutes from here, and had given their driver Google Maps directions to my house. Both exclaimed, "We love all your shows and thought we would come and say hello!"

I tried to be polite. I thanked them for coming all this way and walked them back to their car, trailed by their embarrassed driver. Even so, they persisted, looking back over their shoulders. "We'd love to have a look around, maybe have a glass of wine," they told me.

Wrapped in a tablecloth, I glared at them even as I kept my voice level. "Bye now! Have a lovely holiday!"

People also wander onto the property by accident. Tuscany is a popular destination for keen walkers. When a hiker has taken an unintentional wrong turn, I politely send them in the direction of the public road. But I behaved quite badly when suddenly encountering a stranger inside the villa a couple of years ago.

We were in the middle of a retreat and the guests had just left for a trip to a vineyard for a wine tasting. The staff had gone home for a well-deserved break, and I decided to lie down upstairs for a few minutes' rest. I'd barely closed my eyes when I heard someone shouting, "Hello, hello, hello, help me!" Leaping off the bed, I raced downstairs to find an agitated old man in the middle of the living room.

"I've lost my wife," he wailed.

"Well, she is not in my house," I said, and led him out the kitchen door, pointing to the driveway. I went back upstairs and lay down again, but when I tried to doze off, all I could see was the tear-stained face of a very frightened pensioner. Berating myself for my unkindness, I got up and went to look around outside, but he'd vanished.

I leapt into the massive Defender, a vehicle that easily handles rough terrain, and drove through the upper olive grove: no sign of him. Down towards the pond: ditto. Then I heard shouting. Driving slowly down an overgrown hunters' track, I found him, both arms in the air, calling up to a dangling pair of thick, stocking-clad legs and feet in hiking boots. Climbing out of the car, I came alongside him and looked up to see a lady in her late seventies hanging off the wooded embankment.

"Daphne, just let go and slide down—I will catch you, my dear."

"Hold on," I said, and moved the frail old man aside and took his place. Daphne—crying "Whee, catch me if you can!"— slid onto my shoulders, her tweed skirt stuck in her knickers.

Thankfully I did.

After I'd hoisted them both into the Defender, they told me they were staying at a nearby bed-and-breakfast with their family. They'd been married for sixty-five years and had spent their honeymoon hiking in Tuscany; they'd come back every year since. Daphne, now in the early stages of dementia, had wandered off, which is how Frank had found himself in my living room.

I delivered them both back to the B&B: a safe and happy ending for all.

"Life is either a daring adventure or nothing."
—HELEN KELLER

# We Need a Holiday
# from People on Holiday!

Hans and I have entertained our way through the last six weeks and must now recoup our energy for the fall retreats. In early September, we're ready for our own holiday. And so we head to the beach.

*Why aren't you taking your own advice?* I hear you say.

In September I don't have to. As crowded as the beaches are in August, they are a delight the rest of the year. And now that the crowds have fled, leaving behind stretches of deserted sand and empty cliff-edged coves, I can indulge my love of the sea. I feel alive bathed in the salty air and the vastness of sea, sky and sand. Also, we can't travel far from home this year because of the puppy, so we've decided to glamp in the sand dunes on the Tuscan coast, where we can stay in a fancy tent among the dunes or an even fancier wooden cabin under the umbrella pines.

I am not the camping type: too many uncomfortable memories of childhood holidays spent crammed inside damp caravans. It always seemed to be raining when we went on vacation, which

left us stuck inside, playing endless board games. As the eldest child, I got to sleep on a blow-up mattress under a leaking tent, which I preferred to being squished in the caravan with my siblings, all farting under damp duvets. It was no holiday for my mother, either; she would sob as we set off. How she would have adored a safari-style glamping tent with all the conveniences of a stylish hotel.

Hans and I set out for this much-needed and well-deserved five-day break with one piece of hand luggage between us. The rest of the car is jam-packed with puppy paraphernalia: a dog crate and mattress, a sack of kibble, numerous toys, a first aid kit and puppy treats for the car ride.

I'm looking forward to encountering other dogs on the beach. At the villa, Billie hasn't had much chance to meet canine friends. When we arrive, we are thrilled to meet another dog as soon as we get out of the car—he's staying with his people in a cabin next door. But after some initial bum-sniffing, he turns away from Billie, disinterested. I feel like a mum in the kindergarten playground watching her child be ignored.

I leave Hans to unpack the car and take our puppy for an evening walk to explore the dunes and, with luck, find a four-legged friend. The sun is low, the heat of the day still radiating from the sand, and the only sounds are the rumble of the waves and the seagulls noisily cleaning up the beach. Billie is soon at the end of his extension leash, racing ahead. The dunes are high, and as he crests one, he disappears. Then the pulling on the leash stops. I quicken my step, plastic bag at the ready, expecting that he's paused for a poo. I climb the dune and there he is, standing on top of a bare bottom that is squirming on top of another bare bottom.

Let me pause to explain something. Border collies require lots of mental stimulation and playtime. Billie and I have been practising a game where I get on all fours and he jumps on my back. (This is how I fill my evenings now!) Our fearless puppy has joined in this couple's fun, thinking they are playing another version of our game.

A frantic scuffle ensues as the couple crawls out from under Billie and hauls at least some of their clothes back on, uttering a deluge of profanities in Italian. Then they leg it down the deserted beach, leaving our puppy once again with no one to play with.

> "There comes a time in every woman's life when the
> only thing that helps is a glass of champagne."
> —BETTE DAVIS

# Please Don't Judge Me

Back at the cabin, Hans has already opened the *vino* and pours me a glass as I relay our first adventure on the beach.

We have no plans for the next five days except to read books, hold hands as we walk the puppy, swim in the sea and ignore, as best we can, the to-do list waiting for us back home. In an expansive mood, I decide I will eat and drink whatever I desire. If that happens to be pasta for both lunch and dinner, accompanied by uncounted glasses of wine, bring it on.

Over the following days I work my way through the menu of La Dogana, the rustic restaurant on the beach. It's exactly what you would imagine when picturing a laid-back holiday by the sea—a shack with bleached floorboards, long benches and wobbly tables packed with customers with sand between their toes. The first day I choose the fried calamari and shrimp, the grease cut with a chilled bottled of rosé. Then comes spaghetti alle vongole—a steaming plate of al dente pasta topped with tiny clams. Hans shares his grilled octopus, caught that morning by local fishermen.

We happily pick from each other's
plate. The best dish of the stay is
a lemony linguine with shrimp.
When the days become short
and the winds roar, I often
fall asleep dreaming of this
quite perfect meal.

When we first arrived
in Italy, we turned exploring
the country's delicious cuisine into
a hobby. As the social whirl of restaurants and parties grew, so did
our waistlines, and we asked ourselves how the locals manage their
high-carbohydrate diet and the temptation of Italy's superb wines.
It's rare to see truly overweight Italians. Though many of the older
women living in the countryside do display the roundness of middle
age, the gentrified ladies of the cities are rarely plump. Stroll around
Milan, Florence or Rome, and you won't be able to miss the slim and
elegantly-turned-out women, from teenagers to grand old dames.

I soon realized that if I were to live in this country of culinary delights, I needed some tips. Once I began studying what the
people around me were eating, I realized they rarely demolished
their serving of the traditional pasta dishes that are served at
formal dinners. Instead, they nibbled the corners of a ravioli and
quietly left the rest. When it came to the *secondo*, or main dish of a
meal, they concentrated on the *contorni*—the side dishes—usually
a selection of grilled seasonal vegetables and a simple green salad.
And then they politely ignored dessert.

Hans and I have learned to follow in their footsteps. At home
we live off the bounty from the vegetable garden, alongside plenty
of beans for protein and eggs from the nearby farm. We save pasta

and pizza for holidays and time with friends. The other saving grace that keeps us from packing on the pounds is that there are no take-outs in the Italian countryside, no pad Thai, curries or Vietnamese noodle soups available. (Mind you, I'd kill for a burrito right now.)

We often abstain from booze for months at a time. I would not survive the summer social season without this discipline, but I have to admit I find it extremely hard.

My parents were not big drinkers. They enjoyed a glass of sherry on a Saturday night, and like most middle-class households in the 1970s, they had a liquor cabinet for special occasions. It was under lock and key, but of course I knew exactly where the key was kept—under the far-left corner of the rug in the dining room. Luckily for me, my mother and stepfather rarely offered their guests any crème de menthe, Sambuca, Cointreau or port, a god-send as I'd topped up most of the bottles with water. Lancashire teenagers like me and my pals also never had a problem ordering a drink in a pub. (The only time I've been asked my age when buying alcohol was in Los Angeles, and I was fifty at the time.) As teens out on the prowl of a Saturday night, we'd drink either a warm Guinness mixed with blackcurrant syrup or Babycham, an overly sweet spumante served in a coupe glass with the iconic logo of a prancing fawn. I am not sure if they still sell this once-popular refreshment, but I know the glasses are now sought-after collectors' items. I'd find both tipples undrinkable today, but being bought a Babycham or a Guinness and Black, as it was called, by a hopeful lad back in a pub in Lancashire was the kickoff to an evening out on the town.

In my London drinking days, the nightly house parties were fuelled by cheap, rough Chianti wines that came in straw-covered bottles we turned into candle holders when they were empty. Those bottles once symbolized Italian restaurants everywhere outside Italy: remember the iconic spaghetti-eating scene in Disney's *Lady and the Tramp*? By the time I was an exhausted young mother, my nightly drinking habit was a much-deserved glass or two of wine after screaming at my boys, "Go to bed! It's mummy's wine time."

Today I attempt to drink like an Italian, which means sipping my wine slowly, savouring the flavour and enjoying the moment. But I am a piglet when it comes to a drink. I love everything about social drinking. Heaven is sipping a negroni whilst watching the world go by in the piazza, appreciating the artistic skills of a host mixing the perfect gin and tonic, hearing the rattle of ice in the martini shaker or the pop of a cork. The clink of glasses alongside the laughter of friends eradicates any thoughts I have of giving up booze, but for the sake of my waistline and my overstressed liver, moderation is now my aim.

Drugs are a different matter. They were a constant presence during my London party days, but I have always found them easy to resist. If a spliff was passed around, I passed. I was well aware of the goings-on as friends crammed together into a club's toilet, but I was never interested in putting anything up my nose. It just wasn't my thing. Quite honestly, I would rather buy a new pair of shoes then spend my hard-earned money on cocaine.

I probably shouldn't share this story, but here goes.

I was at the height of my television career. If you flicked through the TV channels pretty much anywhere in the world, I would pop up on the screen in overalls, holding a paint brush in one hand and the hand of a clueless homeowner in the other. In short, I was a recognizable public figure. It was summer and my sons were off travelling with friends before they headed to first-year university that fall. Our production company was closed for a couple of weeks of holiday, and I was lolling around at home with Hans, basking in the wonders of being alone. The weather was sizzling, a heat wave stretching from Montreal to New York.

"I need to get out of the city," I moaned one morning.

Though my little brother was living in the Big Apple, he had a cottage on a lake on the Canada–U.S. border. I knew it was empty. "Let's go to his place," I said.

I messaged him, asking whether it was all right if Hans and I went to stay.

*Of course, it is—just don't make a mess. The key is under the stone by the front door*, he wrote back.

Excited, we threw swimming gear into a bag. I grabbed two steaks from the freezer and a couple of bottles of decent red wine.

A great buddy of ours had stayed with us a few weeks earlier, along with a friend of his whom he was nursing through cancer. As I was about to leave the house, I remembered they'd left their medical "stash" hidden in the back of a kitchen cupboard. It included a tin of "special" cookies and a couple of joints. "Oh, why not!" I giggled and grabbed the lot. I was a middle-aged empty nester running off with my husband for a naughty weekend— I deserved to have some fun.

We arrived at my brother's empty house already high on the thought of the weekend ahead. The Victorian clapboard cottage sat in a cluster of similar homes perched around a shimmering lake. We swam, lit a campfire, grilled the steaks and tucked into the first of the two bottles of wine. As the sun slid behind the mountains,

I brought out the cookies. I had never eaten a weed cookie before. They were stale and tasteless, but dipped in red wine, they added to the thrill of the evening. We ate the lot. Relaxed yet silly, and feeling like we could do anything, we finished off the illicit meal with a joint. Then, what the heck, we smoked the last one. Neither of us are smokers, so there was a great deal of spluttering, followed by side-splitting laughter.

"Let's watch a movie," Hans said.

We staggered inside and rifled through my brother's stack of DVDs, where we found one of my favourite films, Guy Ritchie's *Lock, Stock and Two Smoking Barrels*. Vinnie Jones, Sting and Jason Statham are just a few of the talented ensemble. The movie is violent yet laugh-out-loud funny, music and guns blaring throughout. While Hans futzed around with the DVD player, I raided the kitchen, desperate for something sweet to eat. My brother is known to hoard a British candy called a Curly Wurly—a six-inch length of braided soft toffee coated in milk chocolate. It is beloved by many because of the way the chocolate crumbles off as you chew the toffee. I found his secret stash. Bringing the box of Curly Wurlys over to the white sofa, we snuggled up and settled into the film. There was no sound. We turned it up to the maximum, but for some strange reason we only had the picture. In our happy state, we didn't care. We watched the intense action, lip-reading whilst munching our way through the stolen candy bars. The night was hot and steamy, so soon we stripped off to our now chocolate-stained T-shirts and undies.

About halfway through the film, we heard police sirens. Both of us were confused, since we were watching a mute action film. Hans got up to look out the window. He laughed and said, "This is more exciting than the movie! There must have been a break-in somewhere."

A half-dozen police cars were roaring up the lane, sirens wailing, red-and-blue strobe lights illuminating the surrounding woods.

The phone rang. "What the hell is going on?" my brother screamed down the line from New York. "Are you two having a party? The neighbours have been calling me, and someone's rung the police."

"I know," I giggled. "They're here now, banging on the door, and no, we're not having a party, we are quietly watching a movie. I'll call you back."

Together we opened the door to find three police officers, two of them women who recognized me.

"Hey, we love your show!" They looked up and down our partially clothed bodies smeared in chocolate.

"Hi," I said. "This is my brother's place. We're just watching a movie."

That's when we all realized what had happened. A few weeks earlier, my brother had hooked up loudspeakers to the outside of the house for a lunchtime barbecue. He'd forgotten to reverse the sound to the interior sound system, and so his stoned sister and brother-in-law had blared James Brown and "Zorba's Dance," alongside gunfire, at levels high enough to reverberate through the neighbourhood.

That was the end of my druggy shenanigans: a caution from the three understanding cops, who asked me to autograph their notebooks.

Back at the beach, sunlight spills through the shutters of the cabin as I wake to the early-morning hush. Hans and Billie are still in the land of nod, so I slide out of bed with the same caution I once used to avoid waking a newborn baby. All is quiet around me. Even the cicadas have yet to screech into life.

My emotions run deep as I contemplate the end of this short break together. It seems there is only a heartbeat between the start and the end of summer. My mind drifts to memories of the passing season at the villa. As June blended into July, the gardens and the surrounding land reached their peak, lush and vibrant. Hardy roses tumbled over stone walls and up iron pergolas, gifting us an explosion of apricot, red and white blooms. Agapanthuses, their giant blue heads precariously perched on skinny stalks, lined the walkways in stately splendour. The multicoloured oleander bushes have grown to the size of cars. The lavender was in full bloom in July, but by mid-August the deep-purple flowers had turned a dusty grey, reminding me to begin seeping them in olive oil to make a relaxing massage oil. Now, in early September, the olive groves are carpeted with an elaborate tapestry of cornflowers and yellow-flowered wild fennel that will grow as tall as a man. Thousands of creamy-white Queen Anne's lace, *Daucus carota*, cover the fields. The large, flat clusters of minute flowers resemble tiny parasols at a fancy wedding. Apparently, they are named after Queen Anne of England, who was an expert lacemaker.

For the last weeks of summer, I will rely on the cutting garden for the vases of flowers I place in each room. Fat-headed dahlias and pink and white cosmos will welcome the guests.

Sitting under the gigantic pine trees that shade the cabin, I realize I miss my garden. It's time to go home.

# CRISPY ZUCCHINI FRIES WITH
# SWEET-AND-SOUR DIPPING SAUCE

SERVES 8 TO 10

*As the zucchini apocalypse takes over the kitchen garden, I do get a bit tired of sneaking this vegetable into every dish. I add it to soups, bake it into bread, stuff and fry it, and pop it into salads. Still, there is one recipe that always brings smiles: Tuscan zucchini fries.*

*Parmigiano-Reggiano and zucchini are a perfect marriage, with the cheese's mature tang elevating the humble summer squash. These fries are lovely as a side dish for dinner, but they are even better with a sweet-and-sour dipping sauce and an Aperol spritz.*

*Dipping Sauce:*

1 cup pineapple juice

½ cup packed brown sugar

⅓ cup unseasoned rice vinegar or apple cider vinegar

3 tablespoons ketchup

2 tablespoons soy sauce

1½ teaspoons cornstarch

*Zucchini Fries:*

10 medium zucchini, cut into long wedges

3 tablespoons extra virgin olive oil, plus more
        for drizzling and oiling

1 teaspoon dried basil

Salt and freshly ground black pepper

2 cups grated Parmigiano-Reggiano cheese
    (regular grated Parmesan may be substituted)
2 large eggs, beaten
1 clove garlic, grated
Juice of 1 lemon
1 cup bread crumbs (preferably panko)

Preheat the oven to 425°F (220°C). Oil a wire rack and place on a rimmed baking sheet.

*To make the dipping sauce:* To a small pot, add the pineapple juice, brown sugar, vinegar, ketchup and soy sauce. Bring to a boil over medium-high heat, then add the cornstarch and stir continuously until the sauce thickens. Transfer to a bowl and set aside.

*To make the zucchini fries:* Place the zucchini wedges in a large bowl. Add the olive oil, basil and salt and pepper to taste and toss to coat.

In another bowl, combine the cheese, eggs, garlic and lemon juice. Add to the zucchini wedges and toss to coat. Add the bread crumbs and toss to coat. Drizzle with a little more olive oil.

Arrange the zucchini fries in a single layer on the oiled rack. Bake for about 20 minutes, until golden brown outside and tender inside. Serve piping hot, with the dipping sauce.

# LEMONY LINGUINE WITH SHRIMP

## SERVES 6

*Eating alfresco is always wonderful, but eating overlooking a beach, with the waves rolling in, is unforgettable—everything just tastes better. We tucked into this rich, summery pasta dish several times during our trip to the beach with Billie. I hung around the restaurant's chef every day until he had no choice but to share the recipe for the best pasta I have ever had.*

1 package (1 lb/500 g) dried linguine pasta
3 to 4 lemons
½ cup extra virgin olive oil, divided
Knob of butter
1 onion, finely diced
1 cup freshly grated Parmigiano-Reggiano cheese
    (or regular Parmesan can be substituted)
Salt and freshly ground black pepper
30 cooked shrimp, peeled (omit to make vegetarian)
A handful of chopped fresh parsley

To a large pot of boiling salted water, add the linguine and cook for about 10 minutes or until al dente.

Meanwhile, grate the zest from one lemon into a small bowl. Juice that lemon, along with two others.

In a large frying pan over medium heat, heat a glug of the olive oil and the butter. Once the butter has melted, add the onion and sauté for a few minutes, until softened. Add the lemon zest, lemon juice, Parmesan, Parmigiano-Reggiano and 6 tablespoons of olive oil, whisking until the mixture is thick and creamy. Season to taste with salt and pepper. Taste and, if you like the pasta really lemony, as I do, squeeze another lemon and add some more juice.

In a small frying pan over medium-high heat, heat another glug or two of olive oil. Add the shrimp and toss for a minute or two, until warm.

Drain the linguine, leaving the water that clings to each strand of pasta. Return the linguine to the pot, pour the lemony sauce over the pasta and toss to coat.

TO SERVE: Plate up the pasta, top each serving with five shrimp and sprinkle with parsley.

# TOMATO CHUTNEY

MAKES FOUR 8-OUNCE (250 ML) JARS

*From July to October—sometimes even into November—the tomatoes in the kitchen garden keep on coming. Lucky you, you might be thinking, but coming up with different recipes to take advantage of this bounty can be a challenge. I transform the bulk of the harvest into a basic tomato sauce that I freeze for use over the winter months. But I always set aside enough tomatoes to create my favourite chutney.*

*What I love about whipping up tomato chutney is that it can be made all year round, as the seasonings work their magic even on less tasty supermarket tomatoes. If possible, use a mix of yellow and red tomatoes, the size of golf balls. The chutney is thick and jam-like, and the coriander seeds give it a unique, exotic flavour.*

*This chutney will last in sealed jars in the fridge for about six weeks. Try it with a strong Cheddar or goat cheese on crackers, or add a spoonful to a bowl of beans and rice to liven it up.*

1 tablespoon dried coriander seeds

2 tablespoons extra virgin olive oil

4 cups chopped tomatoes (mixed colours)

2 cups finely chopped red onion

4 cloves garlic, finely minced

1 thumb-sized piece of ginger, peeled and finely chopped

1 red chili pepper, finely chopped (optional)

1 cup packed brown sugar

⅔ cup red wine vinegar

½ teaspoon paprika

Salt and freshly ground black pepper

In a small dry frying pan over medium heat, toast the coriander seeds until fragrant, stirring constantly to avoid burning. Remove from the heat and let cool, then partially crush with a mortar and pestle, if desired (or leave whole).

Add the olive oil to a deep-sided frying pan and warm over medium heat. Add the tomatoes, onion, garlic, ginger and chili (if using). Stir in the coriander seeds, sugar, vinegar, paprika and salt and pepper to taste. Reduce the heat and simmer gently, uncovered and stirring frequently, for 1 hour. Increase the heat and bring to a boil, stirring until the chutney is the consistency of dark, shiny jam.

Spoon the chutney into sterilized jars (see note) and let cool completely before covering with the lids and storing in the fridge.

NOTE: You can sterilize the jars and lids in the dishwasher or, if you don't have one, follow these steps: Wash the jars and lids by hand in hot, soapy water and rinse (but don't dry!). Place the jars on a baking sheet in a preheated 325°F (160°C) oven for 10 minutes. Meanwhile, soak the lids in boiling water. If the jars have rubber seals, boil them separately in a pot of water for about 10 minutes. Lay the jars, lids, and seals on a clean tea towel to cool and cover them with another clean tea towel until you're ready to pour in the chutney.

# APEROL SPRITZ FOR A CROWD

SERVES 8

*There is nothing better to serve to friends on a warm summer's evening.*

Ice
16 ounces (500 ml) Aperol
2 ounces (60 ml) lychee liqueur
16 ounces (500 ml) Prosecco or other sparkling white wine

In a pitcher of ice, combine the Aperol and lychee liqueur, stirring well. Pour into individual wineglasses until half full, then top up with Prosecco.

# Autumn

"And all at once, summer collapsed into fall."
—OSCAR WILDE

# W.H.O.T, or Wine, Hunting, Olives and Truffles

I find it hard to welcome autumn with open arms. Some people tell me it's their favourite season, but to me it feels like the aftermath of a fabulous party I'm reluctant to leave. The summer invasion of family and friends is over for the year. There are no more lazy, wine-soaked lunches, and there's no time for an end-of-day Aperol spritz accompanied by plates of crostini topped with ricotta and apricot, runny burrata, saffron honey and walnuts. Now the real work begins as, with our sleeves rolled up, we tuck into a peasant's lunch of bread and cheese. It's harvest time.

Fall in Tuscany is a season of wine, hunting, olives and truffles— or W.H.O.T. Which also stands for the questions all the expat farmers around here, including me and Hans, are asking ourselves:

*Whot* have I got myself into?

*Whot* kind of harvest will it be?

*Whot* a lot of work!

## W Is for Wine

Autumn is for the hunters and the gatherers. Time to reap the rewards of the land. In Tuscany, the season kicks off with the *vendemmia*, the celebration of the grape harvest. Wine is big business here, and September is a tense time for vineyard owners, whom you will find patrolling the straight lines of their plantings whilst glaring suspiciously at the sky.

The weather can be volatile. The days are still blisteringly hot, yet the cool evenings under clear skies have us wrapping ourselves in shawls. The wine growers' big gamble is with time, holding on as long as possible to start the harvest as the grapes grow juicer and plumper by the day. But a September storm can bring an avalanche of hailstones the size of tennis balls, wreaking havoc in minutes. An unexpected downpour can spoil a dinner party, sure, but it can also badly bruise the grapes, or even wipe out an entire crop. It can take years for a small winery to recover from the devastation of one ruthless storm. Since I moved here a decade ago, Septembers have become hotter and drier, and their storms more violent. The devastation of climate change. This year, when storm clouds begin to threaten in the middle of the month, the vineyards leap into high gear, the fields immediately teeming with pickers in homemade headgear to protect them from the relentless sun.

This is the busiest time of year for the wineries, and for tourists too, many of whom visit the area just to take in the excitement of the *vendemmia*. September also brings the cyclists, both from abroad and homegrown. Italians love the sport, and all month we dodge groups of thick-thighed bikers, gracefully in sync, racing across the countryside—the peloton. Then there are the many disciplined solo riders, who slowly and steadily wind their way through each mountain pass. Who wouldn't both slow down for them and applaud them?

We include a biking day in all our fall retreats. Initially we rented regular person-powered bikes. But the beauty of the scenery was lost as, red-faced, our guests laboured up steep inclines, thighs burning. "These are the famous hills of Tuscany—embrace them!" I would shout optimistically between my own gasps for air. But, usually only minutes into the ride, all of us would give up and climb, exhausted, into the backup vans, panting heavily and clutching our hearts. Although each historic *strada bianca*—white dirt road—that criss-crosses Tuscany offers majestic views, they were impossible for our guests to take in while pedalling under their own steam.

Then along came the e-bike. What an incredible invention— a bike designed so that everyone can take on hilly terrain! E-bikes are nowhere near as elegant as the sexy road cycles with their skinny tires and sleek carbon fiber and chrome frames. But who cares when, aboard this clunky cousin with fat tires and a heavy, battery-laden body, you can explore steep hills and gravel roads with the ease of a professional. When we set out on our first electric bike ride, I found it hilarious to watch a group of middle-aged women effortlessly overtake an Olympic-level, Lycra-clad rider, who stared in shocked disbelief as we waved jovially back at him. I wonder if he is in therapy now.

On retreat biking day, I spend an anxious hour watching our guests—some of whom haven't ridden a bike since childhood, let alone an e-bike—practise changing the gears and operating the electronics. Finally, Pier Giorgio, the patient owner of the bike rental company that supplies us, gives the thumbs-up and we are ready to take off. I rein in my inner hysteria and belt out the final instructions: "Even though these are quiet back roads, you will still encounter other vehicles, such as tractors and tourists in rental cars, who are apt to drive too fast. So keep to single file at all times."

Ignoring me, the women race off, five abreast, chatting about god knows bloody what!

Other things I tend to yell:

"There are no loos, so if you need a pee break, please look for a clump of trees."

"Cindy, that is someone's front yard! Pull up your knickers immediately."

"Do not set off with the assist on high or you will lose control of the bike!"

"Melanie is in a hedge! Can someone stop to help her?"

"Please do not overtake Pierre Giorgio. This is not a race, and we don't want any wrong turns."

"Where is Gillian? She did what? Which farm track?"

And so it goes.

Once the ride has ended at an organic sheep farm, where the guests tuck into a picnic lunch, I let out an enormous sigh of relief that each woman is in one piece. My heart lifts as they beam with joy bordering on the orgasmic. "Best day ever!" they proclaim, and I have to agree. Especially once it's safely over.

This fall's bike day has had us meandering through rolling hills scattered with vineyards, all of which are bustling with the harvest. We've bumped along behind tractors precariously loaded with mountains of plump purple grapes, on their way to become the "nectar of gods," riding over white roads stained pink with grape juice. How is it that the rough, often brutal, work of the wine harvest results in something so elegant, so divine, as a glass of red wine?

The wine world is notoriously snobby and can be intimidating, but since I live in Tuscany, I felt it important to understand the region's dedication to the grape. I am by no means a wine expert (apart from being a champion drinker), but here is a little of what I've learned about Tuscan wine.

At the top of the *vino* ladder you will find one of Italy's most prestigious red wines, Brunello di Montalcino—a rich, garnet red, with an intense perfume, velvety on the tongue. Brunellos are expensive, a treat to savour over a special dinner. If a guest brings a bottle of Brunello to your party, they should be invited back. Marry them if that is a possibility.

Then come the renowned Chiantis, once cheap table plonk but no longer, thanks to enthusiastic and passionate growers in the Chianti region.

Our villa sits in a region of clay-rich, sandy soil that grapevines thrive in. Around here, we produce the "wine of the nobles," Vino Nobile di Montepulciano, a name that evolved from the centuries-long tradition of serving this wine to kings, popes and heads of state. Nobile vines stretch out across the slopes that tumble down around the medieval hilltop town of Montepulciano.

When we bought the property, Hans exclaimed that we could not be true Tuscan landowners without a vineyard. With lofty ambitions and the enthusiasm of newbie farmers, we cleared two acres of land, on which we decided we would plant Sangiovese grapes, the staple of Tuscan wines. Next, we had a high metal fence installed to prevent the deer and the ravenous wild boars from gobbling up our hard work. Using wooden stakes, we marked off twelve straight rows, each a half kilometre long and a metre apart; the stakes would then be linked together with wires that the vines would grow up and along. It took us an entire day to bang in the stakes, with help from a couple of friends. We slept like stones that night, the thud of our hammers reverberating in our tired minds.

The next morning, we headed back to our nascent vineyard, where we were greeted by the lanky figure and jovial smile of our neighbouring farmer, Lorenzo, who was busy hammering in more stakes—lots of them. He is a joy to be around, but he does have an opinion about absolutely everything, from the state of this year's figs to what I am wearing. And now he'd taken it upon himself to add another row of stakes, which would mean another row of vines.

On spotting us, he lunged over to a large plastic cooler by the gate and brought out a bottle of rosé and three grubby-looking glasses. He proceeded to pour each of us a brimming glass of liquid breakfast. We tried to refuse—it was only eight o'clock in the morning—but he wouldn't hear of it. He is a man not to be denied his opinions, his work or his wine. So we drank together while he explained why we needed thirteen rows of vines, not twelve: in Italy, he pointed out, the number thirteen is lucky, associated with the goddess of fertility and lunar cycles. While he insisted that he had no intention of trifling with our farming efforts, if we were to have a successful wine, we *had* to plant thirteen rows.

He was desperately wrong. I should have listened to my own superstitions relating to the number thirteen.

Three years later, we harvested the first grapes and worked with a local producer to make a batch of red wine. "Rough, harsh on the palate, teeth-rotting and gut-destroying" is how I imagine *Wine Spectator* reviewing it. My own review? "Drinkable if served late in the evening, after plenty of the decent stuff has been consumed."

The wine did not improve with each harvest. The following year's vintage of Villa Reniella Classico could cause a hangover bad enough to require a visit to the ER, as well as excessive hair growth on unwelcome areas of the body (or so I've heard).

In the following years, we tried different winemakers and occasionally produced a semi-decent drinkable *vino*, but sadly, a decade on, we now sell the grapes for balsamic vinegar.

No one says farming is easy, but I believe it's always worthwhile to try new ventures. Even if they don't work out, and most don't, the decision to just go ahead and do it can lead you to an unexpected path that wasn't previously on the horizon.

For instance, right after we threw in the towel on our wine enterprise, I got a phone call from the Italian-Canadian owner of a successful winery in the Niagara region of Ontario. He had been at a dinner party the night before and had heard about our dismal failure from a fellow guest, who'd heard about it from a friend's friend who lived next door to someone who'd stayed at our villa. Gossip travels, and sometimes that's good. The owner, Charlie, was now asking if he could help me create a wine—not in Italy, but in Canada—a Debbie Travis brand of Pinot Grigio from his vineyard's grapes. Since women are the main buyers of wine, Charlie felt it would be a rewarding joint venture to have a woman's perspective and create an affordable and flavoursome *vino* together. He suggested that a good first step would be a tour of their facility to taste some of their wines. You only have to ask me once to guzzle free wine and I am all yours.

On a trip back to Canada, I spent an entire day with a large group made up of my team and Charlie's. We gathered at long trestle tables crammed with glasses. Charlie is a large, burly man, always breathless with enthusiasm for the grape. He explained to me that we were looking to make a wine I not only approved of but truly enjoyed.

We got to work.

It was a fascinating experience. First you stare at the wine and check out the colour. Then you smell it, stuffing your nose deep into the glass to appreciate the aroma. He would quiz me. "Can you smell blackcurrant? How about spices? A particular floral? How about liquorice?"

Next you get to taste, the wines coating the tongue with a thousand flavours and textures. This is the bit I failed at. I am a lady, and because I am a lady, I do not spit. In the middle of each table were spittoons. I don't think I have to explain this ugly word or say much about the experience of watching each taster spit out the contents of their mouth into these small communal buckets. I swallowed. By the end of the day, I was carried out of the winery.

I was of no use to anyone. I could barely tell the difference between a Guinness and a fine Scotch. I must have tried a hundred different wines. Due to my incompetence, we decided that Charlie would choose the grape that would produce the Debbie Travis Pinot Grigio, given that he is a professional and a brilliant vintner. Our wine was delicious, sold well and even won international awards.

A few years later, Charlie suggested we go for a Tuscan red, made from grapes grown, picked, crushed and fermented in Tuscany. This time, their team came to me, and we all went on the search for the ideal winery to partner with. We spent a week visiting vineyards dotted throughout the large region that makes up Tuscany. We inspected them, tasted their wines (I'd now progressed to spitting) and chatted with the winemakers. Some of the facilities produced their wines factory-style. Others made them in cantinas situated under their rustic farmhouses, which were filled with hanging legs of meat and dried herbs, and on one occasion the family's washing, drying on the line amongst salamis and hams. At another stop, a stooped, craggy-faced farmer showed us around his dark, musty barn, then, to our delight, offered us a shockingly superb Chianti, which we tasted in the company of a couple of pigs and amongst piles of empty soda cans, glass bottles and what looked scarily like stacks of bones.

Just as in the children's fairy tale "Goldilocks and the Three Bears," these wineries were either too big (meaning too commercial) or too small (meaning nowhere up to the challenge of producing the volume we needed). Some were just too dirty. A few ignored us completely, already overwhelmed by coachloads of wine-tasting tourists.

We needed a partner who was "just right."

By the seventh day, the wine-tasting team was flagging. We began to doubt we would ever find the perfect partner to create a wine to label as my own for customers back in North America. It wasn't only the winery hunt that was getting us down. Tuscan hospitality meant that each winery, no matter how humble, offered us platters of prosciutto, salami, nuggets of aged pecorino cheese and dry bread, plonked on top of wine barrels or dusty tables. Even though we were visiting at least six wineries a day that offered us exactly the same fare, we could not refuse their hospitality.

On the last afternoon of the wine-tasting trip, we met a *contessa*. Widowed and living alone in a rambling villa that had seen better days, she had run her winery for over fifty years. Pleasantly surprised by the quality of the wine, a Rosso di Montalcino, we spent a fascinating couple of hours listening to her tell stories on her shaded stone veranda overlooking the vineyard below, abuzz with workers harvesting her grapes.

She'd been born at the end of the Second World War to aristocratic parents who'd lived in a fifteenth-century *palazzo* on the banks of the river Arno, which cuts the Renaissance city of Florence in half. When the Nazis occupied their family home, they fled to the countryside. Here they'd remained. In her late teens, she met the man who became her husband, a peasant working the family's land. "How he understood the *terre*, and how handsome he was," she said, blushing like the pretty young woman she once was. With her money and his muscle and know-how, they dedicated themselves to building a successful winery.

She told us how helpless her parents felt when the Germans took over their *palazzo*, and about the fear that gripped the people of Florence as Italy's supposed allies blew up every bridge that crossed the river into the centre of the city on what became known as the "Night of the Bridges." There was only one they didn't touch: the famous Ponte Vecchio, or Old Bridge. Apparently, she told us, the German consul to Florence had pleaded with Hitler to leave it be, and so it wasn't bombed.

"Did you know," she asked us, "that during medieval times, the Ponte Vecchio was lined with butchers' shops, fishmongers and tanneries, all of which threw their waste directly into the river?" The stench was horrendous and reached up to the fine villas belonging to the Medicis, the wealthiest family in Europe in those days. The grand ladies could not abide the smell of rotting meat and so demanded that each shop sell only gold and jewellery. It has been so ever since.

At the end of that memorable afternoon spent listening to the countess's stories, drinking her wine and soaking up the view of

the vineyards, Charlie gave me the nod. We had finally found the right bed to lie in—not too big, not too small, but just right. Charlie immediately began to negotiate, but it was not to be. Holding up a bejewelled and wrinkled hand, her eyes moist with tears, the countess told us she was selling everything. She'd only agreed to meet with us for some company.

She laughed at my disappointed face, grabbed my hands and said she would introduce us to a neighbouring vineyard run by her children, who had brought a much-needed modern touch to their winemaking. And voilà, we found our partner. Their production capacity fit the number of bottles we needed to fill the shelves of the liquor stores back home, and the wine was affordable, light-bodied with notes of cherry.

And that is how I finally became a smidgen of a wine connoisseur.

## H Is for Hunting

The start of October has us running for cover, the peace and quiet of the countryside punctured by gunshots, bells and hunting dogs barking hysterically. The season has begun.

Billie is holed up beneath our bed and will remain there for the rest of the day, which is just fine, since walking a dog in the woods at this time of year is not advisable, even though a twenty-kilometre area around us is a no-hunting zone. To make this *abundantly* clear, handmade wooden signs with large black letters that spell out *Divieto di Caccia*—No Hunting—are dotted all around us. This is Italy, though, so that means absolutely zip, *niente*, nothing. At this time of year, even when we're making a dash to our own vegetable garden, it's wise to wave a white flag or wear neon.

If you want to take part in the annual hunt, you need three things: a gun, an Italian hunting dog and a permit. I am not a fan of any of them.

Italian hunting dogs are as far from a cuddly companion as you can get. There is the Spinone, an unfortunate-looking animal in my opinion, wiry and square in stature, bred for its fine nose and tracking skill, not its looks. Then there is the Lagotto, an expert swimmer, the ideal dog for duck hunting. Its woolly coat reminds me of a dreadful perm, so it, too, misses out in the beauty department, but people tell me it does make a good pet. The typical hunting hound around here, though, is neither of these, but a bedraggled, floppy-eared mishmash of countless couplings—a tall, gangly, lolloping dog that reminds me of the stereotypical teenage boy after his first growth spurt. Even the most ardent animal lover will take one look at this ungroomed, foul-smelling creature and back away.

But it's hard to blame the dogs for their appearance and bad attitude when groups of them are penned inside mesh cages for months at a time and only released to roam in hunting season. Running amok, noses to the ground, desperate to pick up the scent of any wildlife that can be shot by their master, they bay and howl with excitement. Adding to the bedlam, the dogs wear bells around their necks to warn the hunters not to mistake them for some unlucky rabbit.

The symphony of hunting season would wake the dead, but luckily not today, as the eighteen women at the wellness retreat, who consumed way too much limoncello last night, have managed to sleep through the racket.

The hunters start the season with small critters: rabbits, pheasant, hare, even tiny birds—basically anything that moves. But when November rolls around, it is man versus wild boar.

Plenty of people in Tuscany oppose the hunt; in Italy, overall, it is a massive, never-ending subject of debate. But no matter how anti-hunt you are, it's hard to champion the *cinghiali*. They are a disaster for agriculture—a wild boar can rip through a vineyard, devouring all the grapes in minutes—and they can be dangerous to people. It's rare for them to attack someone out for a walk, but teams of wild pigs running across roads cause hundreds of car accidents each year. They've even been spotted galloping down the middle of highways and dashing through city centres.

Families of boars have destroyed the lawns around our villa several times, invading in the hours before dawn, tearing up the terrain into one muddy mess. Finally, we succumbed to what we were told was the only solution: an electric fence around the perimeter of the property. We turn it on each evening after the retreat ladies have retired, though I'm still nervous that one of them will stumble into it in the night and get a nasty shock. The good news is that the fence is off for now. Billie the border collie has spread his scent around, peeing on every tree and bush, and the boars are staying clear.

However much these creatures are loathed by farmers and homeowners, they are protected as a symbol of Tuscany—except during hunting season, when everyone with a gun is out controlling the size of the boar population, even in the no-hunting zones.

It is a dangerous sport, and not just for the wild boar. Tuscany apparently has one of the world's worst records for hunters shooting themselves, each other or innocent bystanders. One human a week, on average, gets shot during the season, usually a fellow hunter mistaken for a boar or caught in the crossfire of the hunting frenzy. There have also been cases where some poor bugger leaves home for a leisurely walk only to be shot between the eyes.

Recently a mushroom picker was killed not by lethal fungi but by a hunter's bullet.

The hunters around here tend to be as deranged as their dogs. Most are old and many seem to be partially deaf. It is not uncommon to see camouflage-clad granddads scattered across the hillsides around us, bellowing at each other, oblivious of the fact that they are on private land. Or that they are not allowed to shoot anything at all within 140 metres of a house.

The Carabinieri are in charge of enforcing the hunting laws. Even so, at the crack of dawn each day of the season, the hunters gather on the sides of roads—clusters of pensioners smoking and drinking from flasks of grappa—and the police often join them. They seem to be interested in handing out fines only to people caught without the correct permit—a permit not actually applicable because, as I stress once again, this is a NO hunting zone.

Italy, however much I adore it, sometimes leaves me flabbergasted.


It's the first morning of the last retreat of the year. The sound of gunshots and barking dogs has faded as the hunters have moved farther into the woods. I'm relieved, because yoga has just begun on the wooden platform perched on the edge of the valley. The sun is still low, the autumn light faint, but there's the promise of a sunny day ahead. I grab a coffee and stroll down towards the class with the intention of taking pictures.

Instead of finding my guests in the downward dog pose, I see them running from half a dozen hunting dogs, whose tongues are hanging out with the excitement of chasing something different—women in Lycra pants! Terrorized, we all cram into the nearby massage hut. Once inside the refuge, I call Hans to come to the rescue. "*Subito!*" I scream. Immediately!

Soon, my fearless fighter has shooed away the beasts. The army-fatigue-wearing old men have appeared at the edge of the forest, where they are waving guns, whistling at the dogs and hollering at us. Hard to hear if they're yelling apologies or curses.

Calm and civility reign for the remainder of the day. But that evening we find a dead deer on the doorstep, left as a gift for us, along with a note apologizing for the morning's mayhem. (We re-gifted it to Leonardo, the plumber.)

When it comes to hunting, this country is mad.

### O Is for Olives

By mid-October the wine harvest is over and the vines, now depleted of fruit, become autumnal, their leaves turning a kaleido-scope of gold, brown and fiery red. Now it's time to pick olives, an old agricultural ritual.

Wherever you roam at harvest time, you'll notice olive orchards festooned with what look like fishing nets pinned around the base of each tree. On small farms, or *oliveti*, families and friends hand-pick the olives together, as they have on this land for thousands of years. Ladders lean precariously against the trunks of trees. The thick-stockinged legs of the family's *nonna* dangle alongside gnarled trunks as old as the picker while she drags a fat, wide comb along the branches. The fruit tumbles onto the nets below, where children crouch on their haunches, removing sticks and leaves from the heaps of shiny green, black and mauve olives. It's hard work, but everyone takes part, chatting, laughing and joking as they pick together.

I am often asked why we don't use machines to pick our olives. I answer by pointing at the hills around the villa, higgledy-piggledy with olive trees, many of which were planted centuries ago. The straight lines of commercial groves are designed for machines, but mechanical harvesters are of no use here on these steep terraces.

During the first year we owned the property—even before we embarked on the five-year renovation project—we needed to harvest the fifteen hundred olive trees we'd inherited with the farm. (This number has now doubled thanks to Hans's compulsion to plant more and more trees.)

Olives wait for no one. That first harvest, we invited our children and their pals to come help us pick. We shared stories as we worked, and built bonfires from pruned branches to cook our substantial lunches. I laid the tables with red-and-white-checkered cloths and set out plates of salami with fennel seeds and aged pecorino cheese. We grilled fall vegetables marinated in the first batch of the year's oil on the fire alongside chubby glistening sausages. We toasted thick slices of bread, then rubbed them with garlic, drizzled them with the oil and sprinkled a little coarse salt over the top. As we washed it all down with mugs of rough red wine, all of us agreed these picnics rivalled the finest of restaurant meals.

But our children never came back. Not for the harvest, anyway.

The following year we invited our friends to join in. Funny how everyone we know is so busy at this time of year. Then we held an olive-picking retreat. It was not a productive venture. Hans marched through the trees, muttering, "I wish these women could pick and talk at the same time." Boredom soon set in, our guests finding shopping for shoes in the nearby town much more enticing than stripping the olive branches of their fruit.

This year, as for the past five, Hans and I have been working in the groves alongside a busload of Peruvian migrant workers whom we pay per kilo picked. They chat amongst themselves as they work from sunrise until the daylight expires, stripping the trees of every single olive. When they're done, they move on to the next farm. The olives must not be left to sit or they'll rot, so at the end of every day we rush the full crates to a special pressing facility that deals only in organic harvests. Here, we get the annual thrill of watching our tiny babies be crushed into three thousand bottles of scrumptious, vibrant-green extra virgin olive oil. Liquid gold.

But this morning I lie in bed, wrestling with excuses not to get up. My bones ache, especially my thumbs, from days of combing the branches. "I cannot pick another bloody olive," I moan, "and anyway, the Peruvians are far more efficient than I am."

My phone pings with a message from Melissa, a friend of a friend, who recently cornered me at a party and peppered me with questions about buying a property in Italy. She is now asking if we can meet for coffee. Any excuse not to pick! The meeting place is over an hour away, which means if I drive slowly and we meet for quite a while, I can be absent from the harvest for the whole day.

Leaving hubby, not happy, and puppy, even less happy, and the twenty Peruvians, I speed off into the gentle autumn sunshine.


Italy astonishes. It is impossible to be oblivious to the scenery. Signs of the autumn equinox shine through fields that are now a patchwork of burgundy-coloured soil and the purple clover planted to nourish it—nature's own fertilizer. Uplifted, I feel like a new woman out in the world.

I park on the edge of a small piazza and find Melissa waiting for me at the café. She sits in the shade, and I sit in the sun. Her makeup is a natural look that must have taken hours to apply. She is one of those women who could wear a plastic garbage bag and look chic. That's not what she's wearing, of course. She has tossed on a Chanel cashmere jacket to keep out the nip in the air, and polished boots the colour of chestnuts. I glance down at my chipped nails, filthy Barbour and scuffed shoes; maybe I should have stayed on the farm, where I obviously belong. Though I really enjoy my frothy cappuccino and croissant filled with pistachio cream as my companion sips hot water and lemon.

This afternoon, Melissa tells me, she will be signing the contract to buy a decaying convent on a nearby hillside, to turn into a boutique hotel. Then she's flying over a team of designers from New York. "When I have finished, the Santa Anna will be the jewel of Tuscany," she says, "the best and only place to stay."

I'm happy for her, even a smidgen envious, remembering how glorious it felt to take that first big step towards realizing a dream. Still, as she goes on (and on), I find my eyelids feeling heavy in the sun. I am doing my utmost to stay awake when she says something that catches my full attention. "Apparently, the order of nuns who lived in the convent all died from some dreadful plague," Melissa tells me. "There's a marble memorial to them right where I plan to put the pool. I know you've dealt with all the permit issues, so I wanted to ask your advice. Should I get the builders to knock the memorial down right away? It's so ugly! But what will the local authorities do if they find out?"

"A convent in the hills above San Gimignano?" I ask, shuddering.

I know this place. I visited it with a real estate agent years ago, and the nightmare has stayed with me. I also remember the statue of a nun. How could I forget? I stopped to stare at it as I was fleeing the convent in tears.

It took seven years of searching up and down the Italian boot to find our own rundown ruin. We must have viewed hundreds of properties. My memories of the uninteresting ones have faded. Others have become stories to tell.

There was the *masseria* in Puglia that had a railway line running through the garden. The agent shrugged when I pointed at it. "Never used," he said, seconds before a commuter train to Rome rattled through. Then there was the remote farmhouse in Sicily where Hans was stung by a scorpion and was rushed to hospital on the back of the old farmer's tractor because our rental car wouldn't start.

I fell in love with an overgrown medieval villa on sight and was already redesigning the cavernous rooms in my mind when the agent declared that it was for sale only on condition that the buyer agreed to keep the ninety-year-old grandmother as a tenant. Like our friends who'd inherited the grandfather who taught them how to farm. It sounds crazy, but it's not an unusual scenario in Italy. Also, that picturesque lane you love that leads to the property is often owned by the local farmer and is not included in the price. Buying in Tuscany is a minefield of hidden problems, but with perseverance, patience and a stellar property lawyer, you can make it through.

But nothing I witnessed on our buying odyssey was as horrendous as the once-sacred place this friend of a friend is just about to buy.

My sister was with me when we met a real estate agent in a field adjacent to a small convent on the top of a hill. Before we'd agreed to look at the listing, I'd made the agent swear that the nuns were all gone. *Great view*, I thought as we headed up the hill. The agent told us the Vatican had sold the building a decade earlier to a German couple. As we walked towards the convent, the ancient door creaked open, revealing two old people dappled by the autumn light. They looked just like the sweet, white-haired grandparents you find in a children's storybook. They invited us inside for a cup of tea, but my sister whispered, "I don't like this place. I can't go in there. I'll wait by the car."

Shrugging, I followed the agent and the old Germans into a cavernous hallway with a partial roof and an oak tree growing up through the ceiling. *Okay, so it needs some work*, I thought. The living room was dark and dank, the shutters closed against any daylight that tried to sneak in. The furniture smelled damp to the point of mildew, and the floor was scattered with boxes of files and piles of books. A small, filthy coffee table was laid with refreshments. To be polite, I felt I should take a seat, but I, too, was now feeling on edge. I suggested we continue to look around and have tea later. The agent agreed, thankfully, and we left the old people there as we continued the tour.

Huge oak doors led into a large, windowless prayer room lit by oil lamps. Small benches were strewn around. I shivered—something was not as it should be. Shadows danced around the walls, revealing strange shapes in the gloom. Squinting, I gasped. They were skulls!

"The owner is a collector of bones," the agent explained, her chirpiness somewhat diminished due to my look of horror.

She nudged me towards steps leading to a cellar with a dirt floor. The oxygen levels seemed to thin to the point that I felt light-headed. The only light came from one dusty bulb hanging from the vaulted ceiling. A pathway led through lines of open stone graves. We were in the nuns' burial ground. Later, I found out that the sweet old German sitting upstairs with his wife had been arrested and imprisoned several times for exhuming the bones of the sisters.

I know real estate agents will say anything to sell a property, but what this one said next took the cake. "You're a designer," she said.

"Imagine a thick piece of glass over the open graves, beautifully lit from below. It would make for an amazing floor. Modern furnishings. It could be a spectacular dining room."

I bolted.

I decide to say nothing to Melissa; I am sure she saw what I did, and it has obviously not fazed her. I just pray she doesn't take the agent's advice about the dining room decor!

The next day I am back up a tree. The olive harvest is a herculean task, one that makes us rich only in life experience. And *that* it succeeds in doing. We may have sore thumbs from picking, but there is nothing quite like the sure sense of purpose we feel at harvest time. In autumn, it is what we do: we pick the olives, press them, bottle the nectar and ship those bottles to anyone who wants to taste real olive oil. Then we bask in every compliment that gushes in.

I became aware of the complicated world of olive oil only after we moved here. Much of the olive oil people buy in supermarkets is a blend of low-quality oils from different parts of the world, much the same as box wine. The business of olive oil is fraudulent on an enormous scale that upsets me terribly. A few years ago, I was wandering around a flashy Italian gourmet shop in New York when I came across a lady standing behind a table laden with different brands of olive oils and baskets of bread and crackers, asking shoppers to taste the oil.

"It's just been freshly picked and pressed in Tuscany," she shilled to the small crowd gathered in front of her.

"But it's June," I interrupted.

"Yes," she carried on. "Beautiful June olives from Tuscany—that's in Italy, you know."

"Olives are the size of peppercorns in June!" I shouted back. Then I pointed out that, on the back of the bottle, a label said her product was olive oil mixed with canola.

I was marched out of the shop by a security guard and a beefy guy from behind the cheese counter.

It wasn't until I was an adult that I realized olive oil was meant to be consumed. The only time I remember it being used in our house was to unblock ears. My mother bought the oil in tiny medicinal bottles from the pharmacy. She did sometimes make a vinaigrette, mixing the oil with brown malt vinegar, but she didn't toss it with a salad. Instead, she slathered it over her bikini-clad body while working on her tan, trying to intensify the effect of the stingy northern sun. (We were unaware of factor 50 sunblock in those days.)

Now high-quality extra virgin olive oil, the best from our own and local farms, is part of our daily lives. Each morning we add a teaspoon to a mixture of lemon juice, green tea and cayenne pepper—a bit foul to get down at first, but I promise it starts the day with a kick, and you'll never be bunged up again. I also rub olive oil on my dry legs as a super moisturizer and through my hair as a conditioning mask. We soak salads in it, dip bread in it, cook and bake with it and, of course, marinate dried tomatoes and peppers in it.

We depend on a good harvest, but there have been years when we lost the entire crop to an attack of bugs. Since we don't spray with pesticides, we abandon our trees until the following year.

The harvesting and selling of our homegrown olive oil is truly a labour of love.

—

I have lived my life believing that, yes, I can do it, let's try, and if I fail, at least I have a tale to tell. If our little olive oil business falls apart due to climate change or lack of a market, then we will pull up our socks and move on, poorer, sorer, but happy for what we experienced.

I have had as many failures as successes in my life. The successes pay the bills, but the adventures that have gone truly wrong are the ones that continue to entertain me. There can be much hilarity, along with life lessons, to be found in failure.

In our London years, Jacky and I were continually attempting to top up our meagre income as models with a variety of entrepreneurial enterprises. I've already told you about our market stall selling the pretty camisoles with the pockets dusted with cocaine. That foray into the retail world could have resulted in jail time, but it did not discourage us from trying other things.

Back then, both of us (along with every other young woman in London) salivated over the clothing sold by Browns on South Molton Street, where the likes of Alexander McQueen and John Galliano exploded onto the fashion scene. In the 1980s, it was *the* place to go for the latest must-haves, patronized by ladies who lunch, wealthy foreigners and successful career women. Since Jacky and I were none of the above, we saw only our dreams reflecting back at us from the shop's windows.

A decade before McQueen's edgy ensembles appeared there, the American designer Norma Kamali hit the racks at Browns. Jacky and I stood like groupies in the drizzle outside the store, drooling at the window display. The pieces were as stunning as they were expensive, clothes you'd want in your wardrobe forever: ankle-length skirts made from suede as soft as butter, each a different vivid colour. Under the grey London sky, the Kamali window resembled an aviary of exotic birds.

"Let's go in," I blurted.

Jacky nodded.

Exuding fake confidence, we strolled into the shop, heads held high. Under the snooty nose of a shop assistant, we tried on the skirts. To say they were gorgeous is an understatement. To say they were the price of a month's rent is right on.

An hour later, we sat on the number 22 bus, heading home. Sighing, Jacky stared out over the wet London streets.

"We could make them," I announced. "Look at me, Jack— we could make them. It can't be that hard! Then we could sell them at a fraction of the cost of the ones in Browns."

Our new venture faced several immediate problems, the first being the fact that we had no money to buy the suede. Also, the only sewing either of us had ever attempted was in detention at school. But every predicament has a solution; you just have to search it out or, in my case, ask my mum. She suggested that we presell the skirts and use the money from the orders to buy what we needed to make them.

Not that she necessarily thought we could pull it off. She was brought up at a time when the goal for a woman was to raise children as best she could and make a decent Sunday roast. She was not of the generation who encouraged their offspring to burst through the glass ceiling. Far from it. She finished our conversation with: "Well, if this new venture doesn't work out, do not even think of moving back home—your brother has already moved into your bedroom."

Still, we took her excellent advice and through sheer bravado managed to presell two skirts to a couple of the models in our agency. Cash in hand, we took the Tube to the outskirts of London, to a tannery where they treated the animal skins, dyed them and cut them into lengths. It was a decrepit old factory building, a foul-smelling place, which is why it was on the edge of the city. We bought several metres of electric-blue, lime-green, harvest-gold and lavender suede. Ecstatic, we chirped excitedly all the way home, ignoring the unpleasant whiff of dead animal wafting from the large paper bag across our knees, which was drawing the pointed looks of the other commuters.

Disaster struck the next afternoon. We'd found a paper pattern for a skirt similar to Norma Kamali's in a London department store. We religiously laid out the suede, carefully cutting the pieces on the bias. But when we went to sew them together, as hard as we tried, we could not push our needles through the suede. Bleeding and cursing, we gave up—we certainly didn't have enough money to buy a sewing machine.

But then inspiration struck: we did have enough for a hot glue gun. Firing our new purchase up, we glued the pieces together, even managing to attach the waistbands. Then we invited the two models to the flat to try the skirts on. Success! One loved the bright green and the other loved the lavender. Jacky and I slipped into the gold and blue ones, all of us pairing our skirts with glittery boob tubes.

Resembling a flock of brightly coloured parrots, we hit Soho's Wag Club. It was never easy to get past the doormen there, but this time we handled that hurdle with panache. (Perhaps because we had George Michael with us; Jacky's soon-to-be husband was his record producer.) We hit the dance floor looking fabulous; we were

fabulous. It was a steamy summer evening of drinking and dancing, hot and sweaty in our thick suede skirts, four girls writhing
together to Wham! and Grace Jones.

We danced on and on, and then, in the wee hours, I heard a
scream above the pounding music. I looked around and spotted
Linda, one of our customers, mouth open in shock, hands over her
lacy thong, her skirt in a pool around her ankles. Soon all our skirts
were on the floor. The heat of our sweaty bodies had caused the
glue to let go, leaving us standing in our underwear.

Since this was the eighties, nobody cared a tosh. But sadly,
another prospective career bit the dust. We would never be fashion
designers, but nothing could dampen our entrepreneurial spirit.
A week later we had taken up knitting!


### T Is for Truffle

I knew nothing about lumpy, aromatic, extremely valuable truffles until just before we moved to Italy. A friend bought a small
farm hut in Bergerac, in southwest France. She whitewashed the
stone walls, bought some Ikea furniture, and, voilà, she had an
inexpensive pied-à-terre where she could escape her hectic London
job on the weekends. When she invited Jacky and me for a visit,
we hopped on a flight with one of the discount airlines that had
taken over abandoned air force bases in rural areas of Europe and
offered cheap flights. Super-cheap—I remember that my coffee on
that plane to France cost more than my airline ticket.

While the three of us had a good time together, what sticks in
my memory most from that weekend away is the pig.

We had been strolling across a clearing in a nearby wood when
two men in army fatigues, one of whom was carrying a large sack

and a spade, came crashing through the trees, shouting in French for us to get out of the way. Behind them lunged a humongous pink pig straining at the end of a thick rope, an equally rotund man hanging on to the other end, desperately trying  to keep up. The troupe disappeared into the trees, and we followed. With all their shouting and grunting, they weren't hard to track. Soon we found the three men kneeling around the pig, who was snout-deep in the dank earth. We inched towards them. One of the men looked up at us, smiling now. He waved us over as the fat man shoved the excited pig aside, reached into the hole and lifted out what looked like a knobbly lump of soil the size of a tennis ball. It was a truffle (the fungal kind, not the chocolate). He passed it around to his companions, each man deeply inhaling the earthy scent then uttering an orgasmic sigh. We could smell the slightly funky yet intoxicating aroma from where we stood.

In the local bar that evening, we learned that a truffle that size was worth a pretty penny, given that they were selling for a few thousand euros a kilo.

That was my first and only encounter with a truffle pig and its keen sense of smell. There is one problem with this animal: truffle pigs love to chow down on their priceless finds. Because of this tendency, truffle hunting with pigs in France is a dying art; they are being replaced by dogs. In Tuscany, where the truffles are the best in the world (or so the Tuscans insist), dogs have always been used. Traditionally, the Lagotto Romagnolo, a curly-haired breed blessed with a highly sensitive nose, roots out the truffles from under the oak trees. More often, though, you will see small, wiry dogs that look like a mix of poodle, terrier and spaniel wriggling in cages in the back of vans, raring to be set free to track these treasures.

Truffle hunters operate in a cloak-and-dagger world wrapped in mystery. Many of them work at night, partly because the truffles' scent is stronger then, but mostly to hide from prying eyes. Hunters usually work alone, another way to keep the location of their hunts secret. Think about it. One white truffle the size of a golf ball will bring hundreds of euros from dealers and chefs worldwide, all obsessed with this elusive food, a shaving of which adds an exotic aroma and flavour to a plate of pasta, a soufflé, a wedge of cheese, even a bowl of ice cream. Some of the truffles found around here are sold in local cafés and restaurants for fistfuls of cash, but the best of the best go to dealers who fly them, probably first class, to the finer culinary establishments around the world.

The woods around Villa Reniella are dense, a combination of brush, chestnut trees and ancient oaks. As I've mentioned, people in Italy have the right to roam, which means anyone can walk through your property. I often come across hunters and gatherers picking from God's larder. The Tuscans are born foragers, expert at locating wild asparagus, tiny garlic bulbs, fennel and herbs in the undergrowth. But only a few know where to find the big prize: white truffles. (They are actually black, but when sliced open they reveal tiny white dots, which is where they got their name.) People harvest white truffles from fall through the winter. Black truffles, less aromatic and with no white dots, are hunted in the summer months.

I often spot a couple of rosy-faced sisters, elderly widows from the village, who on seeing me always slide behind the nearest tree and stand very still, like toddlers playing hide-and-seek.

"I can see you!" I'll shout.

They hide not because they are trespassing, but in case the mad Englishwoman intends to compete with them for their lucrative truffle business.

Truffles also figured into the first night we stayed at the villa, a memorable evening forever etched on our souls. We had shovelled out a place to sleep amongst the rubble, laying a mattress on the floor in a room that was habitable—there was no hole in the roof above us. We had the luxury of indoor plumbing too, a bathroom that had been installed in the sixties, with a stained pink tub and a matching loo missing its seat. We'd rigged up a camping stove and found a rickety table and two chairs, and on that first evening we called Reniella home, I boiled a pot of pasta and slathered it in tomato sauce from a jar. We sat down to this simple meal as happy as honeymooners. The gentle evening breeze caressed my bare shoulders, the summer air was heavy with the intoxicating scent of lavender and lemon blossoms, and the valley was spread out below us like a Renaissance painting. Kissed by the final rays of the setting sun, we clinked mugs of red wine, unable to stop smiling, overwhelmed by the depth of our emotions. I had lived this moment in my dreams, and now here we were, feasting on this next chapter.

Before we'd taken the first bite, the romantic moment was shattered. Around the corner of the house lunged an exceptionally tall man decked out in muddy boots and a camouflage jacket, an army satchel slung over one shoulder and a shotgun over the other. He came to an abrupt stop a few yards from us, three barking dogs at his heels.

"*Buona sera.* Welcome to Tuscany. I am Pierpaolo, the truffle hunter," he said, giving us a wide grin. He pointed at his canine companions, as if to prove his point. "*Buon appetito,*" he wished us, then he waved and disappeared into the woods.

Hans looked upset. "I'm not going to allow poachers to invade our land. He's stealing our truffles!"

At that time, we had no clue that anyone with a legal truffle licence is allowed to rummage around on your private land. Hans began huffing and puffing about installing a fence around our hundred acres, possibly adding a few land mines (kidding, I think!). He was still grumbling when the truffle hunter returned half an hour later.

"*Vieni qui*," he called, beckoning us to him.

Hesitantly, we did as we were told. When we got close, he opened the satchel and with large, leathery hands gently pulled out three truffles the size of tangerines. We took in a scent like damp oak leaves, musky yet delicate. He placed all three in my hand. A gift, he told us, welcoming us to the neighbourhood. Then he crashed off through the bushes, followed by the three little dogs. His warmth and kindness completely thawed us. He had given us truffles from *our* land!

Pierpaolo now takes our guests on hunts, but never in our own woods. The location of our truffles is a highly guarded secret, even from us.


At the end of October, the clocks go back. Logs are stacked high to see us through the upcoming winter. The lemon trees in their oversized terracotta pots are dragged one by one into the glass house where they will flourish with new blossoms until early spring. We wave goodbye to the pool as it is covered, leaving us full of summer memories. In the now crisp early mornings, the valley below us resembles a frothy sea dotted with the hilltop islands and church spires that poke through swirling fog.

Sweater weather has arrived and so have the slugs and snails, their silvery trails criss-crossing the stone pathways. They offer endless entertainment for Billie. He nudges and paws their rubbery bodies until I hide the poor things in a hedge. They inspire revulsion in many a gardener for the way they munch through young shoots, roots and tubers. But I let the slug population be. They are nature's recyclers of vegetative waste and are essential for composting.

Hans is maybe less of a fan. The closest I've ever seen him come to totally losing his temper was over a bag of snails.

We'd just arrived at a rental house in France, which our family was sharing with two other families, all excited about the summer holiday. At least, the parents were. My boys were on the cusp of teenagerhood, a terrifying age. They were given to sulks that could sink a ship and sneered at just about everything outside their tight circle of buddies—especially holidays with Mum and Dad. (During one tumultuous weekend break, they'd asked me if they were adopted. I nipped that in the bud by replying, "Do you really think if I had adopted children, I would have chosen you two?" They guffawed and went back to thumping each other.)

The old stone farmhouse we'd rented was on the edge of a town in the region of Bourgogne-Franche-Comté, famous for its Burgundy wine. "Boring" was the first comment from the back seat as we arrived at what looked to me like an idyllic home away from home.

I had blathered on for weeks about the wonders of France, especially the bars and bistros bustling with a nightlife the kids would love. The place was deserted. My elder son scoffed as one octogenarian shuffled past, saying, "That's the nightlife, Mum?"

Happily, there was one thing that put smiles on their faces. Every time they heard the name of the town, they burst into knee-slapping laughter. They took photographs, goofing around in front of the road signs. Most of them feature their pants and boxers down around their ankles, their pimply white bums in the air, their faces hysterical with giggling. You may have already guessed why. You may even have visited the small town of Anus, two hours east of Paris. I do wonder why the town's name has never been changed, since it means the same thing in both English and French. But it cracked up our kids, and their laughing made the miserable holiday bare-able.

The rental house had turned out to be filthy and overrun with mice. On arrival, the other mothers and I set to scrubbing floors and dusting furniture, while Hans escaped to find a phone booth to check in with our television production company back in Montreal. The *cabine téléphonique* was a glass box with a shelf and a phone that had a slot for coins. (I am explaining this in case you don't remember the days before cellphones.) When Hans got through to our receptionist, he was slammed with the news that the offices had been robbed and all the computers stolen. He legged it back to the rental house to tell me and gather any relevant paperwork, and then we headed back together to call the insurance company.

Annoyingly, the phone booth was now occupied by a man wearing the quintessential French beret, his bike leaning against an adjacent wall. I half expected a string of onions over the handlebars to complete the scene. We waited patiently while he hollered down the phone, gesturing wildly. After ten minutes or so, Hans rapped on the window and tapped his watch. With a shrug and a scowl, the Frenchman turned his back on us. Then we witnessed the most peculiar thing. He pulled a large, lumpy brown paper bag out of the satchel that hung around his neck. With a grubby hand, he removed a snail from the bag, held it up, examined it as if checking out a rare gemstone and proceeded to describe the creature in great detail to the person on the other end of the phone. Once he had exhausted the merits of the snail, he plonked it down on the shelf in front of him and extracted the next snail from the bag.

"A fat, juicy one," he bellowed, and set it down. "A muscly, grey-tinged one; a delicate, skinny one; one with a long neck; this one's got a short neck."

As he continued to examine and describe each mollusc, the ones he was done with were journeying across the windows of the phone booth, leaving slimy trails. Only after he had described the last snail in great detail, and settled on a price for the lot with whoever was on the other end of the line, did he toss them back into the bag, exit the phone box and, with withering contempt for impatient foreigners, grunt, "*Eh voilà.*" He rode off clutching his bag of snails, soon to be someone's lunch of escargots cooked in garlic, butter and parsley.

By this time, Hans was apoplectic.

Such was our holiday in Anus.

# TRUFFLE POPCORN

SERVES 4

*During the girls' retreats, if the weather cooperates, we hold an alfresco movie night. (Usually Under the Tuscan Sun—surprise, surprise!) We erect a large screen on the terrace, with views over the valley. Once the light is just low enough for the movie to begin, the truffle popcorn comes out. Decadent, rich and delicious, it's the perfect snack for movie night under the Tuscan stars.*

½ cup finely grated Parmesan cheese
¼ cup finely chopped flat-leaf (Italian) parsley (optional)
4 teaspoons white or black truffle oil, divided
3 tablespoons butter
1 tablespoon olive oil
2 cups raw popcorn kernels
Salt (if you can find truffle salt, even better)

In a medium bowl, stir together the Parmesan, parsley (if using) and 3 teaspoons of the truffle oil. Set aside.

In a large, heavy pot over medium heat, heat the butter and olive oil (olive oil is healthier than the usual canola oil, but you need to stay at medium heat). Test the heat by dropping in six popcorn kernels—once they pop, add all the popcorn and cover the pot. Shake the pot while the corn pops.

When the popping slows down, remove the pot from the heat, add the Parmesan mixture and shake the pot some more.

Tip the popcorn into a large serving bowl and toss some more with clean hands. Season to taste with salt, tossing to coat.

"The secret source of humor itself
is not joy but sorrow."
— MARK TWAIN

# Big Girls Don't Cry

The leaves have faded to brown and drop relentlessly around us. Each sunny day feels stolen, a gift to hang on to, but it is hard to ignore the melancholy that blankets the land. With the retreat guests gone until spring and the wine and olive harvests finished, I should be happy, or at least relieved. But every year, mid-November delivers reminders of a time of fear and heartbreak. Not even tears wash away these November memories.

I had a carefree childhood until my father died. His illness (the details rarely shared with us kids) was a blur, but I remember every moment of the day I found out he was gone.

It was the fifteenth of November, and I was twelve years old. My home was bursting with people. I could hear the doorbell below constantly buzzing. I'd been instructed by a relative I barely knew to stay in my bedroom. I did as I was told. The atmosphere in the house was tense, a fog of despair. It seemed like hours before the comings and goings died down. Finally, my mother appeared, as I'd known she would. She knelt in front of me. She looked afraid.

Holding my hands, she spilled forth words and tears. "Your daddy has died," she said. "I need you to be strong, to be grown-up, to help the others." I was the eldest of her three young daughters. My baby brother was just six months old.

That night we all slept with my mother, who curled up on the cold edge of the bed. I wrapped my arms around my sisters, their sweet breath comforting me even as they whispered their fears. The baby slept beside us in his crib, occasionally fussing and whimpering. We were all too young to understand the magnitude of our loss and how it would affect our lives. I lay awake for hours, listening to my young mother quietly sob. That long and painful night is etched on my soul.

My father was an engineer in a factory that produced the machines that made candies—the perfect job for a man with a massive sweet tooth. Every evening, or so it seemed, his wife and three little girls would gather by the front door to greet him when he returned from work. First he'd swing my mum around, kissing her in an un-British display of emotion. We'd wait patiently for his attention to fall on us, giggling as my mother shook out his pockets. "Now, Bill, show me the wrappers—how many sweets did you have today?" she'd demand, stern-faced, feigning anger, holding back laughter. He'd pretend to cry, hiding his face, all the while winking at his daughters from behind his hands. My father was always a joker, an incredibly funny and joy-filled man.

When they bought their first car, my dad built a wooden garage next to our house. One night, a violent storm demolished it. The following morning, he appeared with a child's drum around his neck. He lined up his young family and, banging the drum, marched us to the pile of debris that was all that was left of the structure. He bellowed orders like a sergeant major and the cleanup began. He drummed his way around the local streets, bringing all the other kids to help. Mum made hot chocolate and warm bread with honey for the crowd. My dad turned a disaster into one of the best days of my life. Who knows, he probably sparked my love of renovation.

His full name was William Anderson Short, which we thought was hilarious since he was over six feet tall. Our favourite bed-time story was about his best friend at school, who also had a silly name, Dad said: Peter Stinkybottom. Dad would tell us in a serious voice that both of them had been teased by the mean kids. Poor, poor Peter; he hated his name so much. He complained to whoever would listen. How could he possibly go through life with a name like Peter Stinkybottom? Finally, after years of his unhappiness, Peter's mother told him he could change his name to anything he desired if it made him smile more. He was over the moon! Thrilled, he changed his name to George Stinkybottom.

You may not find this story funny, but we would roar, lying on the floor with our legs in the air, screaming, "Daddy, tell us again about poor Peter Stinkybottom!"

My father loved food and had an enormous appetite, yet he was rake thin. "Where does he put it?" my mum would laugh. Eventually we found out he was riddled with cancer.

I've always found it impossible to understand that the end of my father's story came so soon. He was a man who had so much to offer. I last saw him propped up in his hospital bed. Wearing my school uniform, I sat on the edge of the bed and tried to cheer him up. He was gaunt and looked so much older than his thirty-nine years. His skin was thin and yellow, the whites of his eyes the colour of corn. So I told him that he looked like a bowl of custard, and he laughed.

My mother was thirty-three when she became a widow. She'd been robbed of a normal, comfortable life. I lost the final years of my childhood, caught in the complexity of grief.

Back then, no one offered bereavement support. There were no easy-to-access survival tools for either my young mother or us kids. When faced with such a loss, the strategy was to keep a stiff upper lip. I was suffocated with grief, but never said so. We suffered in silence, encouraged to pull up our socks, put on a happy face, there's a good girl. There were pats on the back, of course, even the occasional hug. I remember an uncle whispering kindly, "One foot in front of the other and breathe, my dear."

I had no choice but to grow up. Being forced into adulthood was unfair, but the only option.

On the day of my father's funeral, my mum arranged for us to have a babysitter. I begged her to let me go. She told me I was too young, but I broke her resolve with my whining; she was in no fit state to argue with a strong-minded girl. She told me to go upstairs and put on my best dress. I must have taken ages to get ready, because when I came back down, I saw the babysitter playing with my sisters, and my brother asleep in his pram. My mother and all the relatives had left without me.

It is strange what one remembers from a time of trauma. In a spiral of panic, I stood at the bottom of the stairs in my only posh frock, hair brushed to a shine, shoes clean—a child realizing that she was alone. My mother was understandably not thinking straight. It sounds crazy, but I remember questioning my value, a feeling of worthlessness that would stay with me for years. The overwhelming nature of grief is just how solitary it is.

To a traumatized child, nothing feels safe. A therapist's role is to help you create a new secure place, but with no professionals on call, it takes a special person to help a child pick up the pieces, survive and be whole again. My saviour was my mother's mother, Joyce. When she visited, I came alive. As I've mentioned, she lived a flamboyant life, spending half the year in the south of France and the other half travelling to antique markets across England, wheeling and dealing her wares. She resembled that dark, hard chocolate in a holiday assortment box, the one you have to bite hard to get to the soft, squishy centre. She was as tough as they come, but for those allowed to crack her protective coating, she was kind, invaluable—inspiring yet full of common sense. She didn't dwell on the past, especially her own.

She was the illegitimate daughter of a scullery maid who worked at a grand estate on the border of Scotland and England. Her uninvolved father was the lord of the manor. As a baby, she was fostered out to two women named Peggy and Pearl. She told me she'd loved her two borrowed mothers, probably lesbians living quietly under the radar—this was the late 1920s. She remained in their home until she was thirteen, when she was forced to take a job at the manor. High-spirited and determined, she ran away, south to the coastal town of Morecambe.

There are gaps in her story (probably for good reason). But I know she married very young and gave birth to my mother at fifteen. The boy, my grandfather, enlisted in the army and went off to fight in the Second World War. By the time he came home, she had married someone else. Sounds messy, even cruel, but it was common during those turbulent times. I once asked her why she'd married someone when she was already married to a soldier fighting in Europe.

"I got two ration books," she replied.

Joyce grabbed life by the horns. She marched forward, head high, and when things went wrong, she moved on. Not practical when you have children to raise and support, I know. She sent my mother to a boarding school a hundred miles from their home when Mum was only five years old. There she remained until she was fifteen, visiting home just a few times a year. As a mother, I can't imagine it, but it was the norm back then.

Granny was not a motherly type, but she was a role model. She became an animated and passionate local politician, an advocate for women's rights. I have a scrapbook of her cuttings: "Get the woman out of the kitchen!" she would bellow from the pages of local and national newspapers. She was way before her time. My own mother, on the other hand, was blissful in the home, cooking and ironing and raising her children.

After my father died, my sisters and I understood we were to get on with things. As the eldest, I soon learned to make my own decisions, leaning only on myself. On becoming a teenager, I chased the freedom I found hanging out with friends after school and on weekends. Anything to avoid our crowded house and my mother's quick temper. I loved her and my siblings with all my heart, but I found negotiating the complex network of our family relationships too much at that age. I could not wait to leave home. I knew my mother had been dealt a rotten blow, widowed with four children to raise. She lived in fear of not coping, fierce in her resolve to keep the family together. If she failed to put food on the table, we would be taken by the authorities and put into care. She gave the impression of being incredibly strong and capable, but I know how terrified she was.

My mother was beautiful, and (I realize now) lonely. With her thick dark hair, she looked like a young Elizabeth Taylor. She had many girlfriends amongst the other mothers in the neighbourhood, but they were Monday to Friday friends. Come the weekend, she was unwelcome at their dinner parties and soirees. No one wants a gorgeous single woman sitting beside their husband at the table.

Within two years of my dad's death, she'd remarried; I will never know whether out of necessity or love. She chose a good man who helped her raise my siblings well, but he didn't have a big impact on me—I left home two years after he moved in.

My mother died young too, only in her early fifties. My greatest regret is never finding the courage to talk to her about her brave journey. She loved me, and I wish I'd made the time to reassure her that being forced to be independent at such a young age was a gift that defined me.

It's only around the anniversary of my father's death that I allow myself to dwell on the immeasurable sadness I felt as a child, just for a while. Then I shake it off and think of all the good stuff in my life. There is so much of it!

# LANCASHIRE HOT POT

SERVES 4

*This is not Italian fare by any means, but it does have much in common with traditional Tuscan food. La cucina povera means "poor cuisine," peasant food that is simple and hearty, with few ingredients yet an explosion of flavours.*

*There are some smells that instantly unlock happy memories of the kitchens of our childhood. Lancashire hot pot is one that always takes me back. It was my father's favourite, and my mother was happy to please him by serving it; it was a fast and inexpensive meal that everyone ate with gusto. The dish is potato-heavy, not meat-heavy. It's not a lamb stew—the lamb flavours the potatoes. When I make it in the colder months at home in Tuscany, I take great pleasure in seeing the reaction of Italian guests. Dubious at first, they soon become intrigued by the aroma of slow-cooked potatoes, lamb and rosemary. As soon as they taste it, they are hooked. I always worry I've made far too much, but there is never a drop left.*

1½ pounds (680 g) waxy potatoes
(a variety that stays firm when cooked)
1 tablespoon butter
1 tablespoon olive oil, plus more for brushing
1 pound (450 g) lamb leg or shoulder, cut into
1-inch (2.5 cm) cubes, including some fat

*continued...*

3 large onions, thinly sliced

3 large carrots, sliced into coins

2 cups vegetable stock

2 tablespoons Worcestershire sauce

Big bunch of fresh rosemary, chopped (or 2 heaping
tablespoons dried, if fresh is not available)

½ teaspoon dried thyme (or 1½ teaspoons chopped
fresh thyme)

½ teaspoon each salt and freshly ground black pepper

2 bay leaves

1 heaping tablespoon all-purpose flour

Preheat the oven to 325°F (160°C).

Peel the potatoes and cut three of them into ⅛-inch (3 mm) thick slices to use as a topper for the hot pot. Cut the rest into ¼-inch (0.5 cm) thick slices.

In a large, deep frying pan over medium heat, heat the butter and olive oil. Once the butter has melted, add the lamb and cook, turning, until browned on all sides. Remove from the heat.

Cover the bottom of a large, deep casserole dish with a layer of sliced onions, then add a layer of lamb, a layer of the thicker potato slices and a layer of carrots. Repeat the layers until all the ingredients are used up (except for the reserved thinner potato slices).

In a small pot over medium-high heat, combine the stock, Worcestershire sauce, rosemary, thyme, salt, pepper and bay leaves. Whisk in the flour.

Pour the stock mixture over the layers in the casserole dish, tucking the bay leaves in a bit. Arrange the thin potato slices so they overlap slightly on top of the dish. Cover with a lid or foil.

Bake for 1½ hours. Remove the hot pot from the oven and increase the heat to 450°F (230°C). Uncover, brush the potatoes with olive oil and return to the oven, uncovered, to brown the top, about 8 minutes. Discard the bay leaves before serving.

NOTE: Enjoy the hot pot on a chilly day with either some sautéed red cabbage or a steaming plate of peas. Mint jelly is also a yummy accompaniment.

"No one is useless in this world
who lightens the burdens of another."

—CHARLES DICKENS

# What a Hoot!

In December, the gardens around the villa seem to fold in on themselves. They've given up reaching for warmth, resigned to waiting it out until hot sunshine fills the days again. Out of my November funk, I appreciate the chilly, stark beauty of the land. I'm also enjoying having the place to myself.

A couple of guests have just left. They are people we don't know well, old neighbours from another life who'd asked if they could visit for a few nights before embarking on a driving holiday across Italy. They'd arrived dressed for a summer beach party, only to gasp at the cold air and stare in disappointment at the bare branches, the empty terraces void of furniture and the covered pool. Wrapped in blankets, we shared a bottle of *vino* in front of the firepit and listened to their grumbles.

"We thought Tuscany was always hot! Didn't you google it, dear? We watched the entire second season of *White Lotus*, and they were always on the beach. Oh, that was Sicily, right. Well, we may head south to warmer climes."

"Good luck," we shouted as we waved them off. The perfect guests, they'd stayed only three hours! Relieved, we opened another bottle and snuggled up.

This morning I sit at my desk. The weather is dull, but my mood is cheery. Still chuckling at the dismay of the guests finding us in winter clothes instead of lolling by the pool, I hear a strange noise. Scratching? Too loud to be mice. Rats? Oh, please, no!

My desk is next to a modern glass-fronted firebox with a long, narrow chimney. The sound seems to be coming from inside the chimney breast. Screeching like a high-pitched baby's cry accompanies the scraping noise. I bang on the wall. I'm not sure what I expect in return. Maybe: "Hey, how ya doing? I'm just checking out the inside of your chimney . . ."

All is silent.

*I'll make a coffee*, I say to myself, *and maybe whatever's in there will be gone by the time I come back.*

Hans has taken Billie to his obedience lesson. Both will soon return grumpy and ignoring each other. Training our eight-month-old puppy is not going well. Billie's purpose in life is to run and herd. He will herd anything, but his favourites are lizards and women in yoga pants. He does not appreciate an hour spent at the end of a tight leash, with a woman screaming instructions at him.

When I return to the office with my cappuccino, all hell has broken loose. Whoever or whatever is in the chimney is now angry. Violent thuds have been added to the symphony of scratching and screeching. It sounds as if Mike Tyson is beating some poor sod to a pulp. I scream for Luca, who is trimming an olive tree nearby. As always, our beloved worker comes running. (I never know what title he deserves, since he does absolutely everything around here. Perhaps the Latin *factotum*—someone with a diverse variety of jobs—is the most accurate. We depend on him for our survival, basically, everything from picking up guests to rescuing us from the calamity of the day.)

"There is something in the chimney," I shout over the racket.

He opens the glass door of the fireplace. I jump aside to avoid an escaping cloud of soot, but Luca gets covered. Cramming himself as far into the box as a full-grown man can get, he shines the light of his phone up the chimney.

"There's something there," he says, his voice muffled.

*No kidding!* An uncharitable thought, I know.

He takes a photograph and backs out to show me. *National Geographic* would be proud to publish this picture. Staring towards the bright light of the phone is a pissed-off owl. He's only about seven inches high; I am not sure if he's a baby or just a small owl. Angry yellow eyes shine in the dark space, and his horny beak is open in distress. Stuck between the metal damper and the chimney breast, he cannot go up and he cannot go down. Luca suggests knocking a hole in the chimney breast, then sees the horror written across my face at the thought of the repairs. I suggest lighting a fire to smoke him out. Luca says that will kill the owl.

He runs to the kitchen and returns seconds later wearing my oven mitts. "I am going in!" he shouts as if heading into battle. Protected by the gloves, he manoeuvres himself back into the fireplace, arms outstretched. Prodding and squeezing, he elicits a fresh batch of screams from our trespasser—soon matched by Luca's cursing as sharp talons dig in. Then I hear a sound like a champagne cork popping. As Luca backs out, a surprised-looking owl lands with a thump in the firebox and proceeds to topple out onto the stone floor of the office.

At that precise moment, Billie and Hans walk in. We all, puppy included, stare down at the angry pile of sooty black feathers. The owl stares back, indignant at being rescued. Bobbing from one foot to the other, it sneezes, then shivers violently, sending Billie to hide behind a chair. I am tempted to join him. This is an irate and, quite frankly, ungrateful bird.

The shaking releases a cloud of chimney ash, revealing a magnificent blend of russet, gold and snowy-white feathers. Billie inches forward on his stomach, front legs outstretched, bum in the air—the "let's play" position.

"A young one," Luca whispers.

Removing the oven mitts that have saved his hands from being turned into steak tartare, he takes off his hoodie and wraps it around the bird. He carries it outside, all of us following, and places it gently on the soft grass. Still looking annoyed, the owl gives us a farewell nod, spreads its velvety wings and launches, flying with ease towards the forest.

I know I hear it in the dead of night, a monosyllabic call. I like to think the little owl is finally saying thank you.

"Rome! By all means, Rome. I will cherish my visit here in memory as long as I live."

—AUDREY HEPBURN

# *Avanti*
# ("No, *You* Bugger Off")

One last friend has come to stay before the family invades for Christmas. I have been buddies with Marilyn Denis, a beloved television host and radio DJ, throughout our careers. Not only has she invited me to be a guest on her show many times, whizzing up cocktails or dishing out decorating advice to her devoted viewers, but also, for some strange reason, given that it is not really what I do, she has occasionally sent me "into the field" to report on entertainment news.

One of my most memorable excursions on behalf of her show was a press junket for the release of the first *Downton Abbey* movie. I am not an interviewer by any means, but Marilyn and her crew thought I was capable of chatting with the series' stars. So, just before the Covid pandemic had the world hiding indoors, I met up with John, her executive producer, at the Four Seasons Hotel in London. He escorted me to a fancy lounge being used as a holding pen for international journalists. Eventually my name was called, and I was led to a smaller room where the television crew was set up: lights, cameras, action!

My first interview was with Jim Carter, who plays Carson, the head butler, and Phyllis Logan—the series' compassionate Mrs. Hughes. She is as kind and observant in real life as she is in the drama. Noticing how uncomfortable I was in a set-up so foreign to me, she went to get me a cup of tea. Then the three of us, surrounded by the camera crew, talked as if we'd been friends for years. By the time I'd moved on to other cast members, such as Sophie McShera, who plays Daisy, and the creator himself, Julian Fellowes, I was feeling confident enough to enjoy myself.

Fellowes is larger than life, more charismatic even than the characters he creates. He bustled into the room, bellowing instructions to have the set-up changed; he wanted to sit beside me, rather than opposite. I morphed into a giddy teenager as he charmed and flattered, never intimidating despite his full-on upper-class English manner. Could this be a new career for me? Interviewer to the stars? Thoughts to muse on.

Until the next day, when John and I arrived at Highclere Castle, the stately home that had been the location of *Downton Abbey* since the series began. It was a typical bone-chilling December day. Rain lashed the car as we drove up the mile-long driveway to the turreted castle. I had planned to saunter into the great hall like Lady Mary, but security forced us to unload me and the camera gear in a parking lot far away from the grand front door. No umbrella. Mud-splattered, bedraggled and drenched to my undies, I perched on the edge of a velvet sofa in front of a stone fireplace the size of my London house. Gently steaming from the heat of the roaring fire, I interviewed Lady Carnarvon, the true proprietor of the castle, who sat opposite me with five drooling golden retrievers at her feet.

"Get this woman a dishcloth," she instructed a minion.

I was dripping all over her Persian rug.

"Eat," she demanded, pointing to a plate of shortbread biscuits. "You do know you are sitting in the exact spot where darling Maggie Smith, or rather the dowager countess, meets the king of England?"

I told her I did, but I felt more akin to one of the scullery maids.

While I'd loved chatting with the actors of one of my favourite television shows, and felt privileged to be sitting where so much of the action took place, however briefly and soaked to the skin, press junkets are not for me. No way could I survive a steady diet of them. I need to leave entertainment reporting to the professionals.

Marilyn has visited the villa several times and is always welcome, an easy guest who laps up Tuscan life and is a whizz at cleaning up after meals.

This time, with our husbands in tow, we take a car trip to Rome. If you have ever imagined driving through a museum, that's what it's like touring the Eternal City. Though, if you want to take this on, I'd suggest hiring a local driver. With Hans at the wheel, we zoom around the monuments as our guests, white-knuckled, cling to the back seat. Tuscan drivers can be erratic, but the drivers in Rome? *Mamma mia!*

As we near the centre of the city, the madness escalates. Marilyn screams, "It's the Wild West!"

"Every vehicle and pedestrian for themselves," I holler back from the front seat.

—

The first rule when driving in Rome is, there are no rules. (Fines, yes, if the Carabinieri happen to be in your vicinity.) Green light, red light, it's all the same: hit the gas. Road markings? They are impossible to distinguish, having faded to nothing. Street signs? Look up, way up, to the corners of the buildings and you might get lucky.

The cobbled streets were not designed for cars. Chariots, maybe. The local drivers and taxis have little respect for oncoming traffic, or indicating, or pedestrian crossings, or pedestrians themselves. Vehicles weave around each other with abandon. People meander across the streets, barely acknowledging how near to death they've come. Iconic Fiat 500s, the miniscule Cinquecentos, argue with huge coaches filled with sightseers. Scooters are everywhere, nimbly circumnavigating anything and anyone in their way. Even the tourists fling themselves around the city on rented scooters, foolishly thinking they're immortal just because they are on holiday.

Ancient Rome was all about eating, art, drinking, promiscuity and being Roman. Modern Rome is the same. Nothing essential has changed. All around us, people gesticulate, using their hands and fingers to get a point across—a complex completion of what they're saying. Italians gesture for many reasons, adding to the verbal with the visual. If someone is too far away to hear you, or when the words you want to send in their direction are impolite, better to gesture. Romans have made an art form out of using the body to signal emotion, fortify an argument or draw attention to the speaker.

The most creative hand gestures are the insults—an arm sticking out a car window or from the back of a scooter in a variety of positions. Roman drivers are fiery, but it is not your typical road rage, just a form of madness built into the Roman psyche: one hand on the horn, the other signalling to any poor sod who gets in the way.

As we tour Rome by car and on foot, we witness a variety of gestures, as common as breathing to the Italians. Apparently, there are over two hundred different ones, but here are a few I'm most familiar with:

1. Even someone who's never been to Italy might have seen the one that means "What do you want? What do you think you are doing!?" It's conveyed by pressing the thumb against the other fingers of the same hand and gesturing upwards.

2. Hands pressed together in prayer doesn't mean gratitude but "So what do expect me to do about it?" In Rome today we are greeted by this gesture from the maître d' of the packed restaurant that has lost our booking.

3. A hand with fingers in the form of horns means "Get out of the road, you imbecile!" We see this throughout our journey, mostly from our own driver, Hans.

4. A fist knocking the air means "How about a one-night stand?" This one never comes our way, not sure why . . .

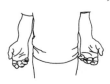

5. Hands held open and cupped upwards in front of the hips, shaking from the wrists. The basic interpretation? "I've had enough of this—my balls are about to explode." Testicles are referred to a great deal in the Italian gestural language.

6. One of the nastier gestures is the *ombrello*, or umbrella, a rude way of saying "Get lost." If a person forms a fist with one hand while slapping the top of that arm with the other hand, he is not being friendly.

7. On a lighter and kinder note, screwing an index finger into one's cheek means "Yummy! That was delicious."

8. Perfection in a meal, an act, an object or a person is indicated by pressing the index finger and thumb together and making an imaginary line.

—

Our days in Tuscany can be simple and satisfying: rescuing a baby owl, an impromptu picnic lunch, picking vegetables from the *orto*, making time for a morning cappuccino in the local bar to hear the daily gossip, curling up with a puppy, and embracing our sons after months apart. This is a life that suits us well.

But it is not all lavender and rosemary. Running Villa Reniella is hard work, physically and mentally, and living in Italy can be daunting at times. The paperwork is endless, the infrastructure of the rules and regulations exhausting. The day Marilyn and her husband set off from Milan, in the north of the country, on their way to visit us, an impromptu national strike was called. No trains, planes, or rental automobiles were available, so they chose the only option other than hitchhiking: a madly expensive, six-hour taxi ride.

A case in point of the frustrations we face here is the saga of our application for a permit to run our wiring underground, rather than on ugly electrical poles. We've been waiting five years. Which is annoying, but as the locals point out, it's nothing compared with the delay on a permit to rebuild the medieval archway in a nearby town, which was bombed in the Second World War. They've been waiting nigh on eighty years.

The retreats are hard work, yes, but they can be mentally draining too. It takes mounds of energy to be the hostess with the mostess. To witness a group of like-minded women come together in this magical haven, where they feel safe enough to share their stories, is a privilege. But I am not a psychologist and have not been trained to stay detached. I've heard so many tales of painful breakups, and they all seem to stick to me. Like the one a guest called

Natalie shared. Her husband of thirty years had left her, he said, because she was well past her best-before date.

I sob alongside those who've been widowed young; they remind me of my own mother. One woman had signed up for a car rally with her husband, both preparing for the trip of a lifetime. He died a month before the event, but she bravely came on her own. She wrote down her daily experiences and turned her little diary into a book that she placed beside his grave.

Then there was Sonia, a widow so distraught she was unable to leave the house after her husband died. She told us she'd been lying half-asleep on her sofa, the television on in the background, when she heard my voice. She looked up and on the screen was *La Dolce Debbie*, our documentary about the renovation of the property. She watched the entire show, then called her grown daughter, who lived down the road.

"Just so you know, I am going to Tuscany to stay with Debbie Travis," she announced.

"What are you talking about, Mom! You haven't even been to the supermarket in five years and now you are going to Italy?" her daughter replied.

We laughed and cried together when we heard her story.

We have hosted women estranged from their children and those who live with the endless grief of losing a child. Our retreats draw exhausted women, heartbroken women, bitter women, frustrated women—sounds like a barrel of laughs, I know, but we do laugh. A lot. And there are also women who come here to live their best life, to ignite their next chapters, to embrace every magnanimous moment that travel offers. They come to the villa to kick-start something—they don't always know what—but they leave us filled with hope and new intentions.

The retreats are a roller-coaster ride of emotions for all who take part in them. I never in my wildest dreams expected that this venture would grow into what it's become, but I am grateful and proud of what we've achieved.

After ten years in Tuscany, we find ourselves in a comfortable rhythm. I do look back, mostly fondly, on my wonderfully crazy twenty-odd years working in television. I have the warmest memories of the people I worked with behind the scenes, and occasionally I miss the wow of walking the red carpet, all dressed up, hair and makeup professionally done. I sometimes even miss the knot in my stomach while waiting for the Monday morning television ratings.

Life now is muddy boots, hair a mess, no makeup and the mundane challenges of a broken tractor, or no yogurt from the farm because it's too hot for the sheep to produce milk, or finding a guest lost on a hike. But as we dedicate ourselves to this tiny corner of our world, we always realize it's also so much more—and never boring, never disappointing.


The Christmas lights appear in mid-December, zigzagging across the *corso*, or main street. They are a marvel, not because of their magnificence—this is not London's Regent Street or New York's Times Square—but because they are beautifully simple. No annual decorating themes, no Disney characters or flying angels. Just a mishmash of coloured bulbs precariously hung from the walls of the medieval village of Montefollonico.

The ladies of the church help the priest install the nativity scene, a tatty collection of clay characters that has seen better days, in the piazza. I'm fully aware that Mary and Joseph were

poor, needing to shelter for the night in a stable and begging for gifts for baby Jesus, but I'm positive they looked smarter than these little painted figures arranged in a manger made from a large olive crate. Most mornings during the Christmas season, the figures have been repositioned by marauding teens in the night: a bottle of beer has been left in the cradle or a cigarette is stuck in Mary's mouth, or she is doing something rude with Joseph as a goat mounts one of the wise men. Boys will be boys, the villagers tut (or smirk). And yet again, the church ladies, their lips pinched, restore the holy scene before the priest gets wind of the bad behaviour.

For the older folk around here, the Christmas season is still a highly religious affair; for them, and the rest of us too, it also revolves around family and, perhaps the true religion of Italy: food.

This morning I dump bag after bag of groceries on the kitchen island. A basket of chestnuts ready for roasting, tangerines fresh from Sicily, sacks of potatoes and a huge turkey to feed the expected crowd. All the vegetables will come from the winter garden. A fellow Brit who lives nearby has picked me up a traditional Christmas pudding in London.

My octogenarian friend from the village, Gabriella, has dropped off a large walnut cake dusted with icing sugar. I look at it suspiciously, as I have done ever since Gabriella offered advice so strange I get a kick out of sharing it with the retreat ladies.

We have several walnut trees on the property. In our first year, I looked forward to the autumn day when they would be ready to pick. I knew that the tree near the greenhouse, especially, was bursting with walnuts, so when harvest day came, I wandered down with a basket to find not a walnut left. Bewildered, I retreated up the steep driveway, where I saw two tiny old women making their getaway with bulging plastic bags and a ladder. Caught red-handed!

When they saw me, they shoved their bags behind their backs like guilty children, then looked up at me with mischievous eyes.

"What's in your bags?" I asked, trying not to sound too cross.

"*Noci*," they said.

"Yes, but those walnuts are from my tree, on my land!" My Italian was even more rudimentary at the time, but I managed to make my meaning clear.

One woman, who introduced herself as Gabriella, went on to tell me a story that is the epitome of rural life here. "We planted this tree when we were ten years old," she said, her voice so low I had to crane forward to hear her. Her partner in crime, Sophia, nodded. "We've been picking these walnuts for over seventy years now, and I make a delicious walnut cake."

*How sweet*, I thought, forgiving them everything.

Then Gabriella gave me an eerie smile and said, in an even softer voice, "If you ever want to kill your husband, use walnuts."

Ignoring my shocked expression, she carried on. (I only caught the gist, so forgive me for fleshing out what she said.)

"There are three parts to the walnut: the nut, the hard inner shell and the leathery green outer shell. When this green shell turns black, it is not only highly toxic, but the poison is undetectable. If you are planning to get rid of your *marito*, mash some into a walnut cake and you have the perfect tool for murder."

They each gave me a wave and, arm in arm, carried on with their slow journey up the driveway. My eyes followed them. Had I really heard what I thought I heard?

Staring down at the walnut cake that Gabriella has been delivering at Christmas ever since, I wonder if this is the year we'll be murdered. But it's too tasty to ignore. I cut a slice and wander outside, munching, as daylight fades and tiny lights pop up in the farmhouses across the valley.

Our peace and quiet is shattered by the invasion of my family. As the kids walk in, Billie treats them to that motionless stare characteristic of border collies as he takes a moment to scan his memory bank. It's been a few months since he last saw them. Then, realizing who these men are, he cries and yelps with jubilation. He leaps on them and they all tumble to the ground, the brothers together again. My heart swells, grateful to have my family around me.

Each Christmas, looking around at us gathered at her table, my own mum would tick us off. Pointing in turn at each person at the festive lunch, she would say, "Tick, tick, tick . . . God, I am happy, everyone is here, everyone is alive."

I feel the same way. Another year has ended, and all of us are in one piece.

We celebrate with traditions from my childhood, new ones we created when the boys were young, and a few Tuscan variations. Instead of a Christmas fir—madly expensive here—I've dragged a potted lemon tree inside and decorated its spiky branches with lights and baubles alongside the lemons. In the middle of the lavishly dressed-up dining table sits the guest of honour, this year's olive oil, an ode to the harvest.

When I was a child, my family always listened to the queen's speech on Christmas Day. (This year it will be the king speaking.) It was not about paying attention to the queen, but about watching my two eccentric grandmothers—my mother's mum, Joyce, and my stepfather's mum, known as Granny Travis. (My father's

mother had passed away the same month he did.) Joyce was anti-monarchy, anti-religion, anti-establishment. Granny Travis was the complete opposite: a good Christian who adored the royal family. My mother would get us all settled around the television to watch the speech, then escape to baste the turkey and overboil the vegetables.

Throughout Her Majesty's address, Granny Travis, dressed in her Sunday best, large-bosomed and ramrod straight, would stand, salute and bow. My beloved Joyce, mad as a box of frogs, would throw peanuts at the television set from her armchair and blow raspberries, then shout, "Pay your taxes, you bastards! Freeloaders!"

From the kitchen my mum would scream, "Mother, please, no swearing in front of the children."

We looked forward to this pantomime every year.


I head to the bathroom to stuff the turkey, so Hans won't see me do it. When he was a small boy in Germany, he was forced to tag along to the butcher with his mother. A traumatic affair. She'd point to a particular fat chicken in the butcher's yard, then she'd walk on to the bakery next door, telling little Hans to bring the fowl when it was ready. He was left on his own to watch the butcher cut off its head, the poor bird continuing to run around the yard, blood spurting, until its last miserable breath. After it had been gutted, plucked and wrapped in paper, the butcher would hand the newly dead bird over to him. Since then, Hans has never been able to look at, let alone eat, a chicken, turkey or pheasant—basically anything with feathers that flies.

During a big family Christmas in Canada, he once walked into the kitchen as I was elbow-deep up a turkey's bottom. Staggering into the mudroom, he slammed into a brace of pheasant hanging from a beam. He fainted on the spot. And that is why I now stuff the turkey in the bathroom with the door locked.

The things we do for love.

# WALNUT CAKE (TORTA DI NOCI)

SERVES 8 TO 10

*I promise that this torta di noci will not kill anyone! When the two old ladies from the village offered me the mindboggling advice on how to murder a husband with walnuts, they suggested using the thick, oily outer coating. Here, we use the nuts. You don't have to be a seasoned baker to have a magical result with this recipe for a safe and succulent walnut cake. It's lovely with a sweet wine or cup of tea.*

*Walnut Cake:*
1½ cups roughly chopped walnuts
2¼ cups all-purpose flour
2 teaspoons baking powder
4 large eggs, yolks and whites separated
      into two mixing bowls
1 cup granulated sugar, divided

*Icing (Optional):*
1¾ cups icing sugar, sifted
6 tablespoons butter, softened
4 tablespoons strong brewed coffee
2 teaspoons milk
¼ cup chopped walnuts

*To make the walnut cake:* Preheat the oven to 350°F (180°C). Butter an 8-inch (20 cm) square baking pan, then line with parchment paper. Let the paper hang over two sides so it will be easy to remove the cake once baked.

In a food processor fitted with a steel blade, process the walnuts until coarsely ground.

Transfer the nuts to a medium bowl and stir in the flour and baking powder.

To the bowl holding the egg whites, add half the granulated sugar. Using an electric mixer or a whisk, beat until stiff peaks form.

To the bowl holding the egg yolks, add the remaining sugar and beat until pale and doubled in size. Gently fold in half the egg whites until there are no white streaks, then fold in the rest of the egg whites. Add the flour mixture and stir gently with a wooden spoon until smooth.

Pour the batter into the prepared baking pan. Bake for 35 minutes, until a knife inserted in the centre comes out clean. Let cool for at least 20 minutes, then run a knife around the edges and use the parchment to lift the cake out of the pan. Place on a wire rack to cool completely.

*To make the icing (if desired):* In a clean mixing bowl, beat the icing sugar, butter, coffee and milk until smooth. Using a palette knife, spread the icing over the cooled cake. Sprinkle with walnuts.

# MOUTH-WATERING CHICKEN CURRY

SERVES 4

*Since Hans cannot eat anything that resembles a winged creature, I have learned to disguise chicken in numerous ways. I've had the most success with curry. This one, my all-time favourite Indian recipe, was shared with me by our expat friends Baal and Mike, exported to Tuscany from Manchester, England.*

*Tuscan food is outstanding, but when you live here full-time it can leave you craving other cuisines. In London, New York or Toronto, there's an immense choice of Thai, Japanese, Mexican—any kind of cuisine, basically. Not so in Tuscany, where traditional food is the norm and there's no option to nip out for Szechuan takeout! Either we cook such dishes ourselves at home or (even better) we get invited for dinner at another expat's house.*

*Still, it's not hard to find the ingredients for curry in rural Italy, as the Italians use many of the same herbs and spices. For example, ground turmeric, a bright-yellow powder derived from turmeric root, is sometimes used here in bread, turning the loaf a sunny yellow. You will find turmeric in most curries, and the same goes for fennel seeds, cinnamon, cumin, mustard and coriander—used in Italy and India in completely different ways.*

> Olive oil, for sautéing
> 2 onions, diced
> 2 cloves garlic, minced
> 1 teaspoon each crushed fennel seeds, ground cinnamon, ground mustard, ground coriander, ground turmeric, ground cumin, cayenne pepper and salt

¾ cup chicken stock
1 can (14 oz/400 ml) coconut milk
1 teaspoon brown sugar
2 boneless skinless chicken breasts, cut into
    1-inch (2.5 cm) chunks
1 thumb-sized piece ginger, peeled and finely chopped
1 small red chili pepper, finely chopped (optional)
1 can (28 oz/796 ml) chopped tomatoes
    (or 4 fresh tomatoes, cored and diced)
1 teaspoon cornstarch
½ cup plain yogurt, heavy cream or whipping cream
1 lime, cut in half
1 bunch fresh cilantro, roughly chopped

In a frying pan over medium heat, heat 1 tablespoon of olive oil. Add the onions and garlic and cook for a few minutes, until softened.

Meanwhile, add a glug of olive oil to a large frying pan over medium heat, then add the fennel seeds, cinnamon, mustard, coriander, turmeric, cumin, cayenne and salt. Stir constantly for a minute or two, then add a splash of stock or water to make a paste. Add the remaining stock, coconut milk and brown sugar.

Once the onions and garlic are softened, transfer them to the large pan and add the chicken, ginger, chili and tomatoes. Stir in the cornstarch and yogurt and bring the mixture to a simmer. Cook for about 10 minutes, then stir in the juice of half the lime.

TO SERVE: Dish out into four individual bowls and scatter cilantro over top. Cut the remaining half lime into wedges for guests to squeeze over the curry. Serve with basmati rice or naan.

"I heard a bird sing in the dark of December.
A magical thing. And sweet to remember.
We are nearer to Spring than we were in September.
I heard a bird sing in the dark of December."
—OLIVER HERFORD

# The Year Ends with Laughter

It is New Year's Eve. From the kitchen, I see the fire blazing in the packed living room. Tonight we are hosting an open house for family and new and old friends, all chatting in a slurry of languages: German, Italian, French, Croatian, and even some English thrown in. The *dolce vita* has brought us all together from many places to wave farewell to the year.

The noise reverberates off the ancient brick arches that once sheltered livestock. The wine flows. I've dusted off a pair of thigh-high black boots and bravely wear a short black dress with a swaying fringe around the bottom. At my age, I probably look ridiculous, but who cares. Hans offers me his effortless smile, mouthing across the room, "My vitamin D." This is his nickname for me—vitamin Debbie—the nutrient he relies on to keep him happy and healthy. His German sense of humour, I know.

I've added a tartan silk scarf because this is also Hogmanay and we've decided to give our New Year's Eve a Scottish theme. My sons wear matching tartan trousers and waistcoats. Others are decked out in tartan ties or checkered dresses—whatever they've been able to dig up in their wardrobes.

I've always been a sucker for theme parties. In England, we call them fancy dress parties. One of my most embarrassing New Year's Eves was the first I spent as a new wife in Canada. We'd received an invitation to a "fancy dress" party from Hans's business associate. The words *fancy dress* were written on the invitation in black and white. I spent days planning and putting together our costumes: Batman and Robin. Hans looked madly sexy in snug-fitting green satin, bare legs and buckled shoes— he was Robin.

We arrived at a flashy mansion and rang the bell. When the hostess opened the front door, buoyant and ready for air kisses, her smile faded fast. She stared at us in our capes and masks, and we stared back at her in her long, slinky evening gown. The party *was* fancy dress—meaning black tie. Undaunted, we circulated, our outfits brightening up the stuffy event.


Minutes before midnight we spill out onto the new terrace. The moon is but a sliver in the velvety black sky—a canvas splattered with stars that shine down on the faces of those I love. The puppy is safely inside, protected from the noisemakers. My two lads are dashing between olive trees, precariously balancing fireworks in milk bottles. Shouts of "Run! Get out of the way!" have them laughing and belting back into the arms of their new wives.

The clock strikes twelve, and someone plays "Auld Lang Syne" as everyone sings along, glasses raised. The old year falls away, the new year says hello.

Hans locks eyes with me. No words needed.

Urgent fireworks burst and streak across the heavens, illuminating this slice of Tuscany, home to farmers and dreamers. I'm happy to be both.

# Acknowledgements

It is a weird process, writing about one's past. I can barely remember what I had for breakfast this morning, let alone bring back the details of my first day at school. But then, often when nodding off to sleep at night, a memory comes flitting in. I need to grab it and immediately jot it down, or poof, it's gone into the abyss. And then one memory just tumbles into another.

I had a lot of fun writing *Laugh More*—especially when I read extracts of the work-in-progress out loud to my grown kids and their partners. There are not enough words in the dictionary to express the joy I felt as they spluttered, guffawed and howled at my stories. They also gave me the courage to share these stories in this book. Thank you Josh, Fiona, Andy and Max.

I am forever grateful to my supportive editor, Anne Collins. This is our fourth book together and she remains passionate and enthusiastic as she gracefully tackles my atrocious grammar and spelling and patiently guides me through the process.

A special thanks goes to Lisa Brancatisano. How lucky I was to have met this spirited Aussie in Florence one day. I soon learned she was an illustrator and when she showed me some samples of her work, I got the tingles. Within minutes, we were discussing the illustrations for *Laugh More* and we have worked together every day for the last year. Her talent abounds. The stunning drawings were incorporated beautifully by the book's designer, Lisa Jager. Thank you, Lisa. I'm immensely grateful, too, to the Random House Canada team and everyone at Penguin Random House Canada. A big thanks to RHC's managing editor, Deirdre Molina, for keeping my book on track. Thank you to excellent freelance copy editor Sue Sumeraj, and to Pamela Murray and Amanda Ferreira for testing and editing the recipes. I'm very grateful to the sales, marketing and publicity team, too, especially Evan Klein, Anaïs Loewen-Young and Emma Ingram. And to the audio team, who went above and beyond to find time in the studio around my crazy travel plans: especially Jaclyn Gruenberger and Martha Leonard.

To my darling Jacky Brown, whose friendship and love spans four decades: *Gracie, amici.* We have had so many hilarious and often dodgy adventures together; I am grateful to you for allowing me to write at least some of them down. No doubt there are many more exploits to come.

I also am grateful to the people in this book whose names I've changed, who have been so wonderful and essential to my life that I didn't want to risk embarrassing them. Hugs to the brave ones who let me use their real names.

ACKNOWLEDGEMENTS

283

I would also like to thank my followers on Instagram, many of whom I feel I know. I really appreciate the way you identify with the many ups and downs that life throws at us and understand the importance of the need to laugh more. This book is for you.

Above all and as always, thank you to Hans. None of this would have any meaning without you.

DEBBIE TRAVIS is an international television host and producer, a bestselling author, a sought-after public speaker, and the designer of the Debbie Travis Home Collection. Her shows, *Debbie Travis's Painted House*, *Debbie Travis's Facelift*, *From the Ground Up*, *All for One* and *La Dolce Debbie*, have been seen in Canada, the United States and eighty other countries. She has authored eleven previous books (eight on decorating) and currently co-hosts a podcast, *Trust Me, I'm a Decorator*, with television personality and designer Tommy Smythe, drawing guests such as Rachael Ray and Marilyn Denis. After stepping back from TV producing, Debbie renovated a thirteenth-century farmhouse on a hundred-acre farm in Tuscany, turning it into a luxury boutique hotel where she offers wellness retreats and classic car rallies, and where she lives with her husband, Hans, and a border collie named Billie.

LISA BRANCATISANO was born in Melbourne, Australia. She moved to Italy in 1993, where she met a local street artist who taught her how to paint with watercolours. Now an illustrator and painting teacher, she works for magazines and fashion houses, as well as taking on private commissions. *Laugh More* is the first time she's illustrated a book. She lives in Florence with her husband, Emiliano, their two sons, Matteo and Thomas, and a border collie named Nami. Go to thistuscanlife.com to see more of her work.